HARDPRESS.NET
HOME OF HARD-TO-FIND BOOKS

Love's Strife With the Convent; Or, the Heiress of Strange Hall
by Edward Massey (Novelist.)

Address:
HardPress
8345 NW 66TH ST #2561
MIAMI FL 33166-2626
USA
Email: info@hardpress.net

LOVE'S STRIFE WITH THE CONVENT:

OR, THE

HEIRESS OF STRANGE HALL.

LOVE'S STRIFE

WITH

THE CONVENT;

OR, THE

HEIRESS OF STRANGE HALL.

BY EDWARD MASSEY.

IN THREE VOLUMES.

VOL. III.

LONDON:

WARD AND LOCK, 158, FLEET STREET, E.C.

250. *p.* 154.

CAMDEN PRESS, LONDON.

CONTENTS.

CONTENTS.

CHAPTER V.

CHAPTER VI.

CHAPTER VII.

CHAPTER VIII.

CHAPTER IX.

CHAPTER X.

CHAPTER XI.

CONTENTS.

CHAPTER I.

FLIGHT AND PURSUIT.

" Haste is needful in a desperate case."
SHAKESPEARE.

DOWN the long avenue the carriage swept, amidst the most dissonant cries. The male portion of the Protestant community vented their joy in hearty English cheers, while the women waved their handkerchiefs, offering up earnest prayers for Ella's safety. The Roman Catholic part of the assemblage were stirred to wrath at a scene which they held to be a desecration of their religion, and loyally responded to the call of Father Francis and the cardinal to make instant preparations for pursuit.

Three carriages of Roman Catholic families in the neighbourhood were hastily brought

B

out, and a quarter of an hour had hardly
elapsed from Seymour's departure, ere the
pursuit began.   Seymour and his companion
passed swiftly down the long avenue, and
turning to the right, made the best of their
way to the turnpike-road, about three miles
distant.   Seymour, who had taken the reins,
pressed his horses, and arriving at the toll-
gate in a few minutes, they found an open
carriage and a pair of capital posters, under
the care of Russell's son ; and also his sister,
who was to accompany Ella as her maid.
They entered this carriage immediately, aban-
doning the reeking horses to the young man's
care.   Seymour drew out a padlock and
chain, and securely fastened the gate.   There
were one or two more in the carriage under
the seat.   " Be quick sir, the flag's going up."
Just as they were on the point of starting
Emperor rushed to Ella's side.   He had evidently taken part in the contest, for his lips
were stained with blood, his hair torn in
several places, and he bore other marks of
rough usage.   Ella begged for his admittance
into the carriage, and Seymour assenting, the

dog stretched himself under the seat. Seymour had concerted his measures so well, and circumstances had so greatly favoured them, that for miles along his destined route he would be warned by preconcerted signals of all the proceedings of his foes.

With eager anxiety he watched the roll of bunting to the head of the flag-staff—an instant's pause, and the black flag was unfurled to the evening breeze. This was the signal of pursuit, and the posters dashed on as hard as they could lay their legs to the ground. The country was tolerably level, but many miles still lay before them. Leaving Wickham behind, they strained every nerve to reach Fareham, where a fresh relay, under the inspection of a staunch old Strange tenant, awaited them at the " Red Lion." The black flag still flew at the mast-head of the first station ; and Seymour, glancing at the second, was anything but gratified to see a red flag fly out from the signal station on Ports-down Hill. This was a token that the pursuers were not more than six miles behind them. " Stop when you pass through the next toll-gate," said Seymour, to the postil-lions.

"Ay, ay, sir."

The next gate was reached; and Seymour alighting, put on a padlock and chain, and securely fastened the gate.

"What's that for I should like to know?" cried the guardian of the gate.

"It's all right, ma'am," said Seymour, "if you will be so good as to let it alone; jump into the carriage and ride a mile or two, and you shall have five pounds."

"What are you going to do with me, sir?"

"Only give you a ride for a mile or two," said Seymour. "You'll be safe enough. There are two ladies inside, and I'll give you five pounds."

The woman's fears vanished at sight of Ella; she complied with Seymour's request, and the carriage rolled onward. "I suppose you are running away with her, sir?" said she, looking at Ella.

"I never tell tales," said Seymour, smiling.

"Never fear me, sir," said the old lady.

"I see you wanted to stop those as is after you—that ere gate will puzzle them."

The old lady was soon set down, and the journey continued at a rapid pace. They were about five miles from their destination when Ella looked impatiently around.

"There he is, Percy," said she.

A lad ran up and put a paper into Seymour's hand; he opened it and read: "The yacht is ready, steam up. Let fly the union as you pass."

Seymour was intimately acquainted with the gentleman in whose grounds stood a signal post, upon which a flag could be seen from the yacht which awaited them. He now descried his friend looking over the palings in some amazement.

"Holloa, old fellow, what are you up to?"

"Saving a young lady from being murdered," returned Seymour. "I must get you to run up your Union Jack sharp, like a good fellow. I've friends who will know what it means. If you see any enemies pass, hoist up a blue flag to the yard-arm."

"All serene," replied his friend, hastening

for the flag. Once more the carriage rolled on, and Seymour looking back saw the Union Jack curling and fluttering in the wind. His spirits rose considerably; but there were still three miles of road before them, and the horses were speeding at a pace at which they could hardly hold on. Seymour called to the postillion to slacken the speed; and the next mile was accomplished more leisurely.

Ella glanced at the friendly flag-staff. "Oh, look, Percy," said she, seizing his hand in her terror. "They are coming." The words were hardly spoken ere the blue flag flew out.

"On! on!" exclaimed Seymour; "kill the horses, but keep them up till we reach the shore," and applying whip and spur the postillions hurried forward. The gig from the yacht was now plainly seen; and from the top of the hill they had reached they perceived the pursuers on horseback. "They shall never take you!" said Seymour, to her terror drawing and cocking his revolver.

"For pity's sake, Percy," she screamed, "put away that deadly weapon."

" Trust me, I will not use it if I can help it," he answered.

The last mile was still to be traversed; the gig's crew saw the state of affairs, and two men advanced towards them; but the pace of the horses was slackening—the poor creatures had done their best—half a mile yet remained. The adversaries pressed on. They were within fifty yards, but a vigorous application of whip and spur to Seymour's horses once more increased the distance between the parties.

One of the postillions now threw himself off to lighten the horses. The benefit was soon apparent; a quarter of a mile now only remained; a loud cheer from the boat's crew reached their ears. The yacht with her flag up for sailing was steaming a few hundred yards from the shore; but cruel fate seemed against them.

" Surrender, or we fire," shouted one of the pursuers, approaching within thirty yards.

Seymour made no answer, but flung Ella on the carriage floor, and bent over her. A few minutes and the " ping " of the bullets whistled round them ; the carriage hood was pierced, but the inmates were safe.

The horses did not escape so well ; the leader bounded with apparently renewed animation a few yards further, and fell dead, But the shore was reached. Four stalwart sailors rushed to their aid. Another moment, and Ella was surrounded by her foes. She shrieked loudly as they dragged her from the carriage, and she found herself in Father Francis' grasp. Emperor, however, bit him so severely in the leg that he quitted his hold with a yell of pain, and turned upon the animal, who despite his exertions pinned him to the spot.

Meanwhile Seymour and a stout Roman Catholic tenant were fiercely struggling ; but our hero, getting his right arm at liberty, dealt his foe such heavy blows, that he was compelled to let him go, and Seymour darted to Ella's side, forcing his way through those about her.

" Back, minion of hell," vociferated he, pointing his revolver in the face of the foremost, "release her, or I send you to eternity." The villain loosed his hold; there was a lull, their pursuers seemed paralyzed. Ella and her maid reached the boat, when, as Seymour was about to follow, Father Francis, who had recovered from his stupor, attempted to detain him. Seymour contrived to free himself, but in so doing dropped Ella's reticule. He would have fought for it, but her mournful entreaties prevailed; one of the crew forced him to a seat——another second and they had quitted the shore. Mr. Stanley rode up at this instant. His language made Ella's blood run cold. Seizing a heavy fragment of rock, he hurled it at them; it fell about the middle of the boat, staving a large hole in her bottom, and she filled fast; one of the sailors, however, doffed his jacket, and crammed it into the hole, and they reached the yacht, though but in a sorry plight. The captain and a gentleman in black received them. Emperor, who had plunged into the sea when he observed the gig pulling from the beach, now scrambled up the ladder, and Ella threw herself upon the faithful creature, dripping as he was, and caressed him heartily.

" Naughty child," said Seymour, " go below at once and change your wet things."

" I'm not naughty, Percy," said Ella, with a pretty pout, throwing on him one of her most witching glances, as she descended to her state room.

Ella and her maid were shown to their cabins, and their luggage was sent down. The gentleman in black turned out to be the Rev. Thomas Lewin, to whom Lord Verdant had given a passage in the yacht. He had not been informed how matters stood, but had merely been told that some ladies and gentlemen from Portsmouth were coming on board.

The yacht steamed past the Isle of Wight and steered for the Belgian coast.

Seymour explained matters to Mr. Lewin, and asked him to perform the marriage ceremony between himself and Ella.

" I should not mind under the circumstances ; but must ask you to write me a letter, just to state that I was not aware you were coming on board ; so that in the event of inquiry, I could clearly prove that I had not connived at your elopement,"

Both Ella and Seymour were good sailors, and they walked the deck for some time in earnest conversation. She consented to become his bride the following day, and Seymour fondly embraced her ere she went down to her cabin.

CHAPTER II.

A WEDDING.

"'Tis He who clasps the marriage band,
And fits the spousal ring,
Then leaves ye kneeling hand in hand,
Out of his stores to bring
His Father's dearest blessing, shed
Of old on Isaac's nuptial bed."

CHRISTIAN YEAR.

THE next day was clear and calm, and the little yacht steamed merrily at the rate of seven or eight knots an hour; Seymour and Ella sat in the saloon while preparations were making on deck for the bridal ceremony.

"I am going to run for a Belgian port, darling," said Seymour. "I am not sure whether under the present treaties if we went to France they might not tear you from me. We will pass through Switzerland, and stay abroad as long as we can. I am not at all sure, as you are only eighteen, it would not be the best plan, after my leave, to go straight back to Bermuda, as Mr. Stanley I suspect is as vicious as ever, and I believe, if he got hold of us, would very likely have me tried for carrying you off, you little pet."

" But what if he did ? " anxiously inquired Ella.

" Why, I might be imprisoned ; as it is, I fear it will fare hardly with some of our gallant defenders ; but I left £200 in Nott's hands to engage counsel for them, in case Mr. Stanley or anybody did take proceedings, but perhaps they will hardly care to do so."

" I thought, Percy, there was some rule against officers being allowed to travel abroad ? "

" So there is, without special permission ; but when you were at Exeter, I wrote an official letter, and said I was anxious during my leave to travel on the continent, and as I should be moving from place to place, I could not give my address ; and I got an answer to say ' I might go,' "

"That's excellent," said she. "I shall never forget poor uncle's cucumber frame, it was smashed to atoms, and the ground, as the newspapers would say, 'presented the aspect of a fierce struggle. There was such a mess," said she, sportively.

"I have no doubt there was," said Seymour, who was in fits of laughter, "I was obliged to hold Emperor, to keep him from Hamilton. I never saw any fellow scamper as he did, and the way he went over the wall beat anything I ever witnessed, except a little Irish boy."

"What was that?" said she.

"Why, my great uncle, Mr. Moilough, built a wall round his garden, and when it was finished, he went carefully round it, and was greatly pleased ; just as he was going away, a little beggar boy passed, and my uncle said, 'Come, my boy, do you think you could get over the wall?' 'Will your honour give me a penny if I do?' said he, in the broadest Irish. 'Oh yes,' said Mr. Moilough ; up went the boy, and down the other side like a lamplighter."

Ella laughed merrily. " He got his penny, I suppose?"

" Oh yes," replied Seymour, " and my great uncle was so disgusted, he had two feet added to the wall; and you can see the marks to this day."

" Now, Percy, I want you to tell me *all* about your proceedings. I never was so surprised as when you met me at the entrance to the church."

" Why, I lulled Mr. Stanley's suspicions entirely by the letter I wrote, pretending to believe you had given me up. I believe the idea that you might be rescued did occur to his dull understanding, for he got Nott, as you know, to bring the Engineers. He ordered them there as a magistrate, and of course *when* there, they raised no suspicion in Mr. Stanley's mind; for Nott had thoroughly bamboozled him by telling him that 'though I was a friend and brother officer, he thought my conduct very bad, and that I ought to apologise.' Then I sent the apology. That not only flattered Mr. Stanley's vanity, but made him grateful to Nott, whom he regarded as an amicable, lamb-like young man, anxious to see all his friends at peace."

" I cannot imagine Captain Nott very lamb-like," said Ella, laughing ; " do you really think that uncle cared for having the apology ? "

" I am sure of it, darling. No man likes to get a black eye and a swollen nose, whether he deserves it or not ; and as in this instance he richly merited a good hiding every day for a year, he was all the more anxious to obtain an apology, so as to be able to say to his friends, ' Well, that fellow Seymour had the grace to send me an apology, deuced gentle-manly worded, too, for what he did,' " said Seymour, mimicking Mr. Stanley's accent.

" Poor uncle Stanley, I wonder what he's about now, and uncle Foll too."

" That's just what I should like to know ; however, Nott will, I have no doubt, write and tell us how matters are looking. I can fancy the fellow sitting in his quarters and chuckling over all the mischief. I should not wonder if he manages to pacify Mr. Stanley, the young humbug. We had a hard race for it, darling.

I was afraid I should have had to use my revolver."

"It was abominable of them to fire," said Ella, "and of uncle to try and sink the boat. I suppose you would have been justified if you had fired also."

"It would very much depend in what light the affair was received. I doubt it ; for though an unlawful act was done in forcing you into the convent, it is questionable whether I ought to have carried you off. At all events, I am not going to risk your safety in the slightest degree, and shall write and lay the whole business before counsel, and see what they recommend. Now, darling, the great event of our life is to happen this morning. I must go and see whether they are ready on deck.

The Rev. Thomas Lewin soon appeared, and conducted Ella to the deck of the yacht ; and, transferring her to the charge of the captain, who was to give her away, she and Seymour stood before the capstan, round which an ensign was wreathed.

In her simple morning dress, a wreath of

orange blossoms confining her hair, on the broad ocean, far away from relatives and home, surrounded by the strange sailors who, in their Sunday attire stood, round hats in hand, did the young heiress plight her love to him who had so long and earnestly done battle and striven for her; and Seymour, as he clasped his trusting bride to his heart, felt that the years of care and pain he had endured for her, could now be dreamt away in an hour. On the fourth day they arrived at their destination. Seymour and Ella bade a hearty farewell to their companions, and left £100 for distribution amongst the crew. The party, now reduced to Seymour, Ella, her maid, and Emperor, went to the hotel he had arranged with Nott, where they were to adopt the *nom de guerre* of Graham. A letter, and the *Hampshire Telegraph* were awaiting them; Seymour pounced upon the former, while Ella contented herself with the newspaper.

Nott's letter was brief, it merely mentioned that " Mr. Stanley was still furious, but as far as he (Nott) was concerned, he had convinced him that the way affairs had turned out was not owing to him."

"Did I not tell you so, Ella; I never saw such a fellow." Nott went on to say that Mr. Stanley was evidently bent on mischief, and enclosed a list of wounded and missing on the tenants' side, which was not a light one. Seymour, however, felt a malicious joy at hearing that the Roman Catholic body had suffered much more severely; and was gratified to hear that the only person Mr. Stanley would prosecute, in a legal point of view, was his precious self. Indeed, most of the Protestants who had taken part in the fray had, as the yankees frequently do, "skedaddled" for a time. Nott wound up with good wishes for every description of happiness.

The *Hampshire Telegraph* gave a graphic account of the whole business, but declared the fugitives had proceeded to Paris.

"Not if we know it, Mr. Editor," said Seymour. "Don't you wish you may catch us in Paris; no, my friend, we are going down Switzerland."

One of Seymour's first cares was to send

an advertisement of his marriage to the *Times*
and *Morning Post*; and, this over, he and
Ella walked out and ordered their wedding
cards.   Neither of them approved of the " no
cards " system.

They spent the afternoon in preparing the
list of the friends to whom cards were to be
sent, and in conjecturing Mr. Stanley's fury
at reading their wedding in the *Times*.

" We'll send cards to Mr. Stanley, I
suppose ? " said Seymour.

" Percy, how *very* naughty you are
to-day," said Ella.   " Of course we shall do
nothing of the kind.   Uncle's angry enough ;
and our sending cards would make him
ten times worse.   I shall write a penitent
letter," said she, looking archly at him.

" Well, my own, do as you please.   He'll
have the pleasure of seeing our wedding in
the *Times*.   Don't forget to send cards to
Miss Ffrench."

" The dear creature ! no.   I won't forget
her ; and I should like to send her a poem
I've been composing.   She is one of my best
friends," said Ella, " and she deserves it."

"Saucy little creature!" said Seymour, attempting to catch the poem from her. "What's it all about?"

"It's my farewell, sir; and I call it 'The Bride's Farewell.' Here it is;" and she read—

"THE BRIDE'S FAREWELL. *

"Farewell, farewell, though the sea be lone,
    And the bark be very frail,
And though resting-place hath the ocean none,
    Nor sleepeth for ever the gale.

"Though borne for aye on the rolling tide.
    I must pass o'er a measureless sea,
I charge ye to cast your fears aside,
    Nor weep, Oh fond hearts for me.

"For I leave not alone the haven of home;
    Nor trust to my own weak hand,
To steer my bark through the breakers' foam,
    Or to row to the distant land.

"I have chosen a guide whom I love so well,
    That my heart has no room for fear,
Though heavy and dark be the ocean's swell,
    And the rock-bound coast be near.

"Through the rage of the storm, through the sultry calm,
    I shall still find one by my side,
Who has sworn to preserve me for ever from harm,
    My lord, my protector, my guide.

---

* From original unpublished MSS.

" Nor look we for aid of earth alone,
  For far in the distant land reigns One
  Who claims us.   For whom we were signed His own,
  When the journey of life was scarce begun.
  And in His strength we dare to tempt the sea
  ' Of Time slow widening to Eternity.' "

CHAPTER III.

PLOTTING AND COUNTER-PLOTTING.

"Oh how will crime engender crime! throw guilt
Upon the soul, and like a stone cast on
The troubled waters of a lake,
T'will form in circles round each succeeding round,
Each wider than the first."

COLMAN THE YOUNGER.

WE must now, in spirit, waft ourselves back to the time when Seymour's and Mr. Stanley's quarrel took place, and even glance again at the solemn midnight meeting.

Before that assembly had been convened, the idea of rescuing Ella by force had occurred to Seymour; and, finding that those who possessed influence amongst the volunteers would lend their aid, and further inquiry having satisfied him that the volunteers would only be too glad of the opportunity to render Ella help, the plans had been concerted by Seymour and Nott.

The former had carefully gone over the whole of the route they afterwards travelled. Relays of horses had been provided, and no suspicion was excited, as he had carelessly let fall, when making the arrangements, that he had a bet to complete a given distance within a particular time. The small carriage in which he and Ella quitted the grounds he had purchased a few days before; and he and Nott had devoted some hours to bolting thin steel plates round the traces, and twisting thongs of leather round the chains, which he used as reins, to preclude the possibility of their breaking or being cut.

Two nights previous to the ceremony—having ascertained Mr. Stanley was from home—the list of the names of the volunteers being ready, Seymour and Nott arranged the parts they were severally to play.

They numbered sixty; and, partly from accident, and partly from a desire to excite their imagination, Seymour and Nott decided to give the different parties high-sounding names, and had drawn for that purpose on a well-known incident in French history.

They met at seven p.m. in a secluded field, on the bank of the river, and the two friends divided them into five parties.

"These ten," said Seymour, reading out their names, "are specially honoured by being styled 'Miss Sinclair's guard.' Your duty will be to surround her the instant I give you the signal in the church, by waving my handkerchief, or by giving you distinct orders. You are to take no part in any fighting, but content yourself with shielding off any blows that may be aimed at you, and draw Miss Sinclair, as soon as possible, to the door. Whatever happens, she is not to be left for one instant."

The party then passed in succession by Seymour and Nott, each repeating in substance what he had been told. They then quickly dispersed, and passed as noiselessly as possible to their homes.

"The next ten are named the 'Reserve Guard,'" continued Seymour. "On receiving orders to advance, you are to come forward, and defend Miss Sinclair and her party from any attack—using your discretion as much as possible, to disable, without inflicting severe injury on those you fight with. The next fifteen I consider the 'Young Guard.' Your duties will be similar to those of the 'Reserve Guard.' Above all, work together, and don't allow yourselves to be separated. The next twenty-five are distinguished by the title of the 'Imperial Guard.' I hope that, without your assistance, I shall be able to complete the deliverance of Miss Sinclair; but if your aid is invoked, remember," said he, raising his voice, "that the Strange and Rockley Imperial Guard never advance but to victory. I shall only call upon you if absolutely necessary; and let your advance be the signal to all to re-form their broken ranks, and fight their very best—nay, their better than best. Upon your conduct, two days hence, depends the happiness or misery of Miss Sinclair— even, perhaps, my own life; for I have sworn that in death alone will we part. If you lose, remember, too, that the Strange and Rockley properties pass into the hands of the priests, and your chance of remaining here will be but small."

In the meantime Mr. Stanley was resorting to strong measures. The scene was in the abbess' room at the convent. Ella was alone with her, and Father Francis and Mr. Stanley in the passage. Ella was in mute despair; for she had just finished perusing the draft of a letter, which the abbess had desired her to write out.

" I will never write such an abominable, cruel lie," said Ella, firmly.

" Shall I tell you what will be done if you do not ? " said the abbess, sternly.

Ella bowed assent.

" You will this night be conveyed away to an Italian convent of the strictest order. Even *I* would shudder to go through the tortures and penances that will be inflicted upon you. Be wise ; and do as you are told."

Ella was in despair. " God help me," she murmured.

"I will give you half an hour," said the abbess, " to copy out this letter ; here are paper, pens, and ink," and she sat down at the table.

Ella glanced round the room. The remains of breakfast were in a corner ; one chance remained. "I will try to write it if you leave me here alone," said she.

"Oh, very well," said the abbess, grimly, and stalked out of the room, closing and locking the door.

Ella glanced around ; she was satisfied none beheld her. She advanced to the side table, there was milk in the cream jug ; she dipped her pen in it, and wrote across the inside of the sheet :——

"DEAREST PERCY,——
      "They have made me write this letter ; "but I love you as when I told you so in the " long walk."

Then wiping her pen, and waiting till the milk was dry, she dipped it in ink, and copied out the letter :——

" MR. SEYMOUR,—

" Upon careful consideration, and with
" regret for your sake, I must decidedly
" say that all must be at an end between
" us. I am persuaded that it is my voca-
" tion to enter upon this most holy life, in
" which so many pious women have lived
" and died. I can there pray for you, but
" you must regard me as one that has passed
" away from earth. In the retreat which I am
" about to enter I shall be free from worldly
" thoughts and cares. It is your duty to
" forget me. Farewell.

" ELLA SINCLAIR."

This note was sent by a special messenger
to Seymour's hotel. Nott was with him at
the time, and was puzzled at the language
Seymour uttered. " It is a forgery," said
he at length, with an angry curse, and
threw it to Nott.

" It's not a forgery," said Nott, carefully
scrutinising it. " I don't believe she did it of
her own free will ; no, I know Miss Sinclair
too well."

" I should like to have Mr. Stanley and
Father Francis here for five minutes," said
Seymour.

" Not a doubt you would ; but it would be
more to the purpose to be five minutes with
Miss Sinclair ; do you remember that naval
expression ' giving a black dog for a white
monkey ? ' "

" No," said Seymour, bitterly ; " I remember nothing of the kind."

" It's no use cutting up rough, old fellow ;
you'll get nothing by that move.　Just you sit
down, write an apology to Mr. Stanley, and a
letter to Miss Sinclair, telling her that you
entirely acquiesce in her views."

Seymour made a sudden rush at the fire,
upsetting the table in his eagerness.

" The devil ! " said Nott.

His friend burst into a savage laugh, and
held his letter to the fire ; gradually the words
Ella had written came out.

" Ho, ho ! " said Nott ; " well, we have a
precious set to deal with, to be sure ; it's all
the more reason for you to repay them in their

own coin. By the way, how was it you did not perceive that writing before?"

"Because it was written in milk."

Nott gave a prolonged whistle, and Seymour explained matters.

"Miss Sinclair seems up to a thing or two," remarked he.

"I taught her this," said Seymour, looking guilty; "but I had no other resource. I thought all sorts of things would be said against me, but I never dreamt of all this mischief."

"Nor I," said Nott, musingly; "we had better not talk any more, but you must write your apology and letter."

Seymour took his penholder from his waist-coat pocket, and wrote his apology:—

"My dear Sir,—

"The terms of Miss Sinclair's letter at "once point out that I was labouring under a "misconception, and having now ascertained "that fact, I hasten to offer you the only re-"paration in my power—a most ample apology "for the conduct I was betrayed into towards

" you, and which I infinitely regret. I feel sure
" you will, however, sympathise with me ; and
" as I am not to be permitted to lead Miss
" Sinclair to the altar, for the holy rite of matri-
" mony, I have a strange fancy, which I trust
" you will not refuse me, to see the last of her,
" and to be near and support her through the
" ceremony of entering upon her noviciate.

" I remain,

" Respectfully yours,

" PERCY SEYMOUR."

A messenger took this composition to the Hall, and a few hours subsequently returned with Mr. Stanley's reply :—

" DEAR MR. SEYMOUR,—

" When a gentleman has done wrong,
" sees his error, and acknowledges it, all the
" past should be overlooked. I accept your
" apology. I am glad to find you have per-
" mitted your good sense to resume its sway
" over your understanding. Under the cir-
" cumstances I feel much regret for your
" position, and accede to your request. If you

" are at the avenue leading to the church,
" about noon, your desire shall be fulfilled.
" Do not take it amiss if I tell you in confi-
" dence that Miss Rivers is much attached
" to you.

" Yours sincerely,
" WILLIAM STANLEY."

" The battle is won!" shouted Seymour.
Throwing the letter to Nott, he proceeded to
stand on his head, and perform sundry extraordinary antics.

" Don't be an ass, Seymour," said Nott,
looking up.

" I have not the smallest feeling in common
with that quadruped, my dear fellow. But I
find it necessary to give vent to my feelings
somehow, and your quarters are a trifle
confined."

" Well, you will have plenty of opportunity,
I fancy, on Tuesday. Mr. Stanley is greener
than I fancied him."

" He *is* an ass, if you like; he thought I
should forget all about Ella. That's all bosh
about Grace," said Seymour, noticing Nott's

rising colour; "she quite comprehended that we were to flirt, on the understanding that nothing was to come of it."

"Did you tell the young lady so?" said Nott, dryly.

"I don't exactly know what I said, but she understood it well enough."

"I should like to know, as a matter of curiosity, how you contrived," said Nott, lighting a cigar. "One never knows the position one may be in. What did you say or do?"

"Well, I said nothing direct; but I told her on our first acquaintance that I loved Ella."

"Not a bad way either," said Nott. "You are one of the coolest hands with whom I have the honour of being acquainted."

Seymour made a mock heroic bow, and they separated for the day; Nott going to arrange the signals which were to be shown from the various flagstaffs, of which, for a *consideration*, they had acquired possession for the next three days; and Seymour to arrange definitely for the yacht which was then lying ready for sea in Portsmouth Harbour. For,

be it known, that he had availed himself of
the Bermuda introduction; and though the
friend's engagements precluded his taking
part in the execution of the scheme Seymour
had contrived, he had, with great kindness,
placed his yacht entirely at Seymour's command.

Seymour now met him by appointment,
and the concluding arrangements were entered
into.

"She is already provisioned for a cruise of
a month," said Lord Verdant. "I suppose
she had better steam round to Hill Head
about two p.m., had she not?"

"It will do if she is there by three, but not
later," said Seymour; "and the boats can put
off when they see us coming."

"I think they had better, if the weather be
fine, be on shore in waiting; you may be run
hard you know," remarked his lordship.

"Very well. Do the people on board know
anything?" inquired Seymour.

"No—I thought it better not," replied
Lord Verdant. "They have the strictest
orders to do as you tell them, and I distinctly

said, if they saw you in any difficulty, they were to render all aid; I rather think they fancy you are an unfortunate fellow who has been spending rather freely, and is in consequence pursued by bailiffs."

"Well, I have no objection to their belief," said Seymour, laughing.

"If you are able," continued his friend, "let a Union Jack be hoisted on the signal staff as you pass. You shall have my horses ready for you at Wickham. My groom will be with them, and the under-groom will be waiting for them at Fareham; and the two stable lads will act as postillions."

"I think the arrangements are perfect," said Seymour, as he conned the paper upon which the heads of the organization had been written.

Seymour returned to Nott's quarters, where he packed a portmanteau and carpet bag, also a couple of boxes of dresses and other requisites for Ella, and despatched them that evening by Nott's valet.

"How do you know the dresses will fit?" asked Nott.

"Oh, when I thought matters were leaning this way, I got one of her old dresses, and have had the others made accordingly. Besides, when once away, with money in both pockets, we can procure all requisites."

"Well, you deserve success, I'm sure; it will be a desperate business if you fail."

"I can hardly do that," said Seymour, "except I am betrayed; and they who know the secret have everything to lose and naught to gain by splitting."

Seymour slept soundly, and the next morning dressed himself carefully, concealed a small revolver under his waistcoat, taking also a large pocket knife. Nott drove him to the church, where he left him, the 'observed of all," while he proceeded to the hall. When the *cortège* arrived, Seymour, who stood at the avenue gate, quietly advanced, and Ella relinquished Mr. Stanley's arm, and took that of Seymour. The rest we know.

Mr. Stanley held several conferences with Father Francis at Strange Hall, the week succeeding Seymour's departure, and his rage hardly knew bounds when he received a note in Ella's handwriting, and tearing it open, found a penitent letter that bewildered him.

" Curse the fellow," muttered Mr. Stanley, between his teeth, " I'll do my best to keep him out of the Strange property." Throwing the letter in the grate he took refuge in the *Times*; but it seemed that all that morning had combined to annoy him, for almost the first paragraph that met his eye was—

" On the 14th of June, at sea, on board Lord Verdant's steam yacht *Undine*, by the Rev. Thomas Lewin, Captain Percy Seymour, Royal Engineers, eldest son of the late Honourable George Seymour, to Ella, only daughter and heiress of the late Sir Arthur and Lady Sinclair, of Strange Hall, and Rockley Park, Hants."

" Curse the whole lot of them," roared Mr. Stanley, savagely. " I'll be even with them yet ! " and he hastily left for Strange Convent, and then taking the express for London, spent some hours closeted with his solicitor.

CHAPTER IV.

TOUR IN SWITZERLAND.

> " Above me are the Alps,
> The palaces of Nature, whose vast walls
> Have pinnacled in clouds their snowy scalps,
> And throned eternity in icy halls
> Of cold sublimity, where forms and falls
> The avalanche—the thunderbolt of snow.
> All that expands the spirit, ye appals,
> Gather around these summits, as to show
> How earth may pierce to heaven, yet leave vain man
> below."   BYRON.

" ELLA, this is a horrid hole; I vote we go on to Switzerland," said Seymour one day as they were about to sit down to breakfast.

" Yes, darling, do," said Ella; " I want to see Switzerland very much," and she rushed to the window.

" Ella, look what you've done, you mischievous creature," said he, turning round after a short interval.

Ella hastily looked to where he pointed; lo she had left the water pouring out of the urn, and the breakfast-table was now saturated. Seymour rang the bell, and a waiter with a most impenetrable expression of countenance, removed the cloth and wiped the table.

" They won't forget it in the bill, Miss Extravagance," said he, and he was correct; for when that document was called for, fifteen shillings was charged for " damaged table and cloth."

" What an imposition," said Ella, peeping over her husband's shoulder at the bill.

" Well, pet, we shall have to pay and look as pleasant as we can, and depart for Basle."

They did so accordingly; and three or four days of easy journeying brought them to that quaint old town, over which its ancient cathedral stands sentry.

The river flowing past their lodging, surging and eddying through the country, sounded very pleasant to the tired wanderers; and on its banks they sat brooding, and consulting over English scenes. They had taken lodgings in a cottage at once retired and comfortable in the very midst of the characteristic scenery of Switzerland. From their retreat they made many excursions, watched the setting sun gilding with glorious tints the old towers of the cathedral. Then they would look on the Alps which lay behind them like a vast sea whose billows had petrified, and watch the dying light paint their snowy tops with rose tints, and dye with gorgeous rays the valleys, vineyards, and towns resting below in peaceful obscurity. Thus much of their honeymoon was dawdled away.

"Well, Ella, I think we'll go straight back to Bermuda anyhow," said Seymour one day, "and allow the Strange and Rockley revenues to accumulate, while the lawyers keep a look out upon that precious guardian of yours, and see if they can frighten or coax him into terms."

"I should like to see the scene of your flirtations, sir," replied Ella, in a saucy tone, "and to Bermuda we will go, with all my heart. How long leave have you now?"

" About three months and a half, puss ; we
can have some more weeks on the continent
yet."

They walked out as usual one evening
amongst pasture lands, cottages, and cattle ;
and ascending a cliff that overhung the river,
sat down upon the soft grass.   The declining
rays of the sun, tinged with gold and purple
clouds, amidst which the beautiful colours of
the rainbow irradiated a gloomy portion, the
low eddying of the river hastening on its
course, and the echo of its " swirl " on the
banks broke the silence of the evening air.
A few tiny boats skimmed gently over the
slightly curling waters, their snowy sails
forming a pleasing contrast to the braided
blue of the river.

" Whither shall we bend our steps from
this, Ella ? " said Seymour.

" Oh please take me to Lucerne.   I so want
to see the monument to the memory of those
noble Swiss who so heroically perished in the
defence of the French monarchy."

" We'll go there by all means ; it is a noble
incident—when all had forsaken and fled from

the French king, a hired band of mountaineers stood by him, and sealed their devotion to his cause by their life's blood."

" Oh had they marked the avenging call,
    Their brethren's murder gave,
    Disunion ne'er their ranks had mown,
    Nor patriot valour desperate grown
    Sought freedom in the grave."

As Ella trilled these lines in her rich contralto voice, Emperor, who was as usual lying at her feet, gave a low growl.

" What's the matter, poor fellow," said Seymour, patting him ; " has she frightened him with her singing ? "

" I'm sure there's some one near," said she, looking alarmed.

" Robbers, perhaps," replied he, laughing ; " don't look so frightened, pet."

At this juncture Emperor rose up and sniffed the air.

" It's Father Francis !" ejaculated Ella. " He'll take me from you !—what shall we do ? "

" I'll help him to a piece of lead if he cuts

any capers of that description," he answered, drawing from his pocket his small revolver, which he had judged best to have constantly about him; " but how do you know it's Father Francis? Surely your terror is deceiving you."

" No, no, Percy," said she, " I saw his face peering from behind that bush as you patted Emperor. Please come home."

They rose to return. As they did so a rustle amongst the trees was heard, and Father Francis and two men in disguise stood before them.

" Villain, you have decoyed that lovely dove from her home—" said Father Francis with a theatrical air.

" If I have," retorted Seymour, " I am going to keep her who is mine, or die in the attempt; I've five men's lives here," and he held up his revolver significantly, " and I'll die hard."

" Daughter, are you his wife? " said the monk, in an austere tone.

" Of course I am," replied Ella, " and if you will look in the *Times* of the 18th of

June, you will probably see the announcement."

"I did you wrong in thought Captain Seymour. I wish you both well. You were always charitable and good, Mrs. Seymour." He raised his cap courteously. His companions followed his example; they turned, and were lost to sight in the adjoining thicket.

"I don't like that party at all, with his honeyed speeches," said Seymour in a musing tone, "and I vote we quit this to-morrow."

"Very well," said Ella, "a few hours will do all my packing. But what a queer thing Father Francis finding us out."

"He's after no good," said Seymour; "but he'd better not play any tricks here."

They took the train the next day and were whisked along the iron road to Lucerne.

"We've missed seeing the convent of Königsfield, Ella—I should have taken you there before we quitted Basle. It was founded, I believe, by a woman who was notorious for her cruelty—Queen Agnes of Hapsburg. Amongst other atrocities, to revenge the murder of her husband, she had an innocent man stretched on the rack where he lay for three days and three nights, his wife standing by his side. He died of course, and the wife died of a broken heart at Basle. Afterwards this queen built the convent, and lived in it, and for all I know may be in your saints' calendar."

"Please don't Percy; I can never bless you enough, my darling, that I now see clearly those things which destroyed my peace. There are indeed among the saints of the Church of Rome those who have no business to be considered saints at all; why, St. Thomas à Becket is known by every one who has studied his history to have been a disturber of the peace of the country, and St. Dominic, who is a great saint of the Romish Church, is the cruel wicked man who founded the Inquisition, which is supposed to have murdered one hundred and fifty thousand Christians in thirty years."

"Horrible!" replied Seymour; "I cannot comprehend how any reasonable creature can imagine that he, who was such a wholesale butcher, could have any part among the people of that Saviour who came to save life. He is amongst the number of advocates in the Litany of the Saints, is he not, Ella?"

"Yes, indeed; and so is St. Francis, who would probably, had he lived in these times, been put in Bedlam."

"What did he do, Ella?"

"Read his history, Percy, and you will know."

"I would much rather you would tell me."

"I would much rather not," she smilingly replied; "go and look after the luggage, and I will stay upon the platform with Emperor to take care of me."

They found a suitable hotel at Lucerne, and were soon seated at a repast—cool Swiss beer, fresh strawberries, honey, and a variety of other good things.

"I wonder what Father Francis really wanted?" said Ella, at length.

"I can scarcely perceive; but if I catch

him prowling near us again, I'll set Emperor at him, and he'll scamper, I'll be bound. I am only sorry I did not do so the other day."

CHAPTER V.

SEYMOUR'S ILLNESS.

" See the wretch that long hast tost,
On the thorny bed of pain,
Again repair his vigor lost,
And walk and run again.
The meanest floweret of the vale,
The simplest note that swells the gale,
The common air, the earth the skies,
To him are opening Paradise."   GRAY.

THE hours of their wanderings passed
joyously by, until one evening Seymour com-
plained of acute headache, and in the course
of a few days was seriously ill. Ella, alone
in a strange country, roused herself to act
on this occasion, and telegraphed to Captain
Nott, the only person she could rely upon, to
assist her. That officer came from England
without an hour's delay. He brought with
him a medical man—a brother of Seymour's
friend Fordbrad. He at once pronounced

Seymour's illness to be scarlet fever, and ordered Ella out of the room; but the girl, brought up as she had been in the lap of luxury, and only in late years bending her will, not without resistance, to those around her, positively refused to obey, and in the long hours of delirium watched unceasingly by her husband's bed. The doctor had endeavoured to talk cheerfully of hope, but even while the words fell from his lips, Ella did not believe him; she had frequently witnessed illness among the cottagers of Strange and Rockley, and felt Seymour had sunk too low to rally from the insidious disease. Long had the delirium now lasted; boyish scenes and doings in the far land of the past, with thoughts and fancies relating to Ella, were mingled in wild confusion in his ravings. His cries and moans had terrified the Swiss household. They had fled from the cottage and declined to enter it while the doleful sounds of sickness rung through its walls. One evening Ella noiselessly drew aside the curtain: the bright beams of a setting sun flung their radiance over the sick man. He was strangely altered; his parched and feverish lips and gleaming eyes appeared as if they hardly belonged to Percy Seymour. Yet while there was life there was hope; Ella sat on; a dreamy unconsciousness seemed to hover around her; a favourite text, " I will never leave thee, or forsake thee," reverted to her mind; wearied with her long watch, she fell asleep. She dreamed she was once more at Strange—she had entered the chapel just as service commenced, but she was so greatly occupied in ascertaining whether Seymour was there or not, that she paid but little attention to the service. As her thoughts thus wandered, the calm form of her mother suddenly appeared—she told her she was mocking the Being she came to worship, and showed her in an instant the thoughts which pervaded the breast of each member of the congregation. Many were, indeed, far re-moved from prayer. One man was thinking of his flocks and herds, another of his worldly occupations; one young lady was wondering whether she would be permitted to go to the next Fareham ball, and another was ponder-

ing whether Lord ——— was going to propose
to her or not.   Children, apparently absorbed
in devotion, were conjecturing who would
receive this or that prize at school, or specu-
lating upon some amusement they had been
promised.   Others there were who thought
of what pastime the coming week would
bring them; and few, alas! seemed thankful
for blessings past, or earnestly asked for
guiding light for days to come.   A slight
movement of the invalid awoke Ella, and she
poured out his medicine which stood on a
little table near her.   He took it without a
word.   Her mind naturally reverted to her
dream which was fresh in her thoughts, and
she prayed, as perhaps she had never before
prayed, for her husband's life.   A holy calm
fell over her; she felt she could almost resign
him if God so willed.   Days of suspense and
sorrow passed away, but Seymour slowly advanced in strength, and was able, when the
time for his departure to Bermuda came
round, to undertake the voyage.

Before they quitted the Swiss mountains
and valleys, the whole party visited, and

glanced hastily through the Abbey of Königsfield, where tradition tells Albert of Hapsburg
was assassinated.

"You remember those lines of Mrs. He-
man's, don't you, Percy? You forgetful creature," she added, as he shook his head. "I
took so much pains to make you learn them."

"Say them then, puss; perhaps they'll
come again," and Ella repeated—

"A peasant girl that royal head upon her bosom laid,
   And shrinking not for woman's dread, the face of death
      survey'd.
   Alone she sate.   From hill and wood low sunk the mourn-
      ful sun,
   Fast gushed the fount of noble blood.   Treason his worst
      had done.
   With her long hair, she vainly pressed the wounds to stanch
      their tide;
   Unknown, on that meek humble breast, imperial Albert
      died."

They soon arrived in Paris, where they
intended to stay a few days.

"You'd better get an extension of leave,
old fellow," said Nott to Seymour. "Bermuda will hardly do for you yet."

"I've had so much leave, I don't like asking for more."

"Well," remarked Nott in an absent tone, "some people are very obstinate."

"Do you mean your remark to apply to me?" asked Seymour.

"If you consider the cap fits, take it by all means, my dear fellow, put it on and wear it; but, indeed, when I spoke I was thinking of an old gentleman's moustache."

"Well, you're a queer fish; out with the anecdote, I daresay it's a racy one."

"It's simply this," said Nott. "Before moustachoes were allowed to be worn in the Infantry, an old fellow was in the habit of shaving *upwards*, the consequence was, that when he permitted his moustache to grow, it came straight out from his face, and not all the power of bandoline would keep it in its place."

"Ha, ha, ha," said Seymour, "you are a good fellow, Nott, to amuse me; but seriously, to Bermuda I must go, if it's only on her account," looking at Ella.

"Well, I'll say no more, I've no doubt it's all for the best."

Seymour and Ella, still under their pseudonym of Mr. and Mrs. Graham, returned to London, and taking the express from King's Cross, soon reached Liverpool without any hindrance on the part of Mr. Stanley or his agents.

Just before they quitted the continent, Seymour received a letter from his lawyer, in reply to the points he had asked information upon. He learnt that his marriage was perfectly legal, and that there was no occasion for the ceremony to be performed over again. " I should, however, under all the circumstances detailed," the lawyer wrote, " advise you not to return to England for some time, as by a recent Act of Parliament it is made an indictable offence to take away or detain any woman, being under the age of twenty-one years, out of the possession and against the will of her father or mother, or of any other person having the lawful care or charge of her, with intent to marry her. The offender is considered guilty of felony, and on being convicted, is liable to a term of penal servitude, not exceeding fourteen years, and not less than three, or to be imprisoned for any term not exceeding two years, with or without hard labour. At the same time, the course of my experience goes to prove that it is very hard to get a jury to convict upon such a charge, and that the facts must be clear to sustain a prosecution under the act. The fact of Miss Sinclair's having been treated with cruelty, and an attempt made to force her into a convent, would be almost certain to cause any jury to consider the affair a love match, and not to convict."

"By Jove, Miss," said Seymour, "see what's going to happen to me. You little goose," he added, noticing her terrified look as she glanced over the letter, "we are going back to Bermuda."

CHAPTER VI.

RETURN TO BERMUDA.

"O'er bog, o'er steep, through straight, rough, dense or rare,
  With head, hands, wings or feet pursues his way,
  And swims or sinks, or wades, or creeps, or flies."
                                        MILTON.

THEY at length embarked in the *Arabia,* and landed in Bermuda two days before the expiration of Seymour's leave.

Their adventures had not reached that colony, and they received a warm welcome from old friends. Seymour found a great many changes. The regiment had left. Fordbrad had, however, been permitted to remain to hold a local appointment. Paymaster Fitz had quitted his regiment, and was in Bermuda. These two old friends were greatly pleased to find Seymour had succeeded in his enterprise, and he had much gratification in introducing them to Ella.

The heat was getting very oppressive, and the English residents found with dismay that vessels with yellow fever patients on board were not only permitted to land in the Bermuda waters, close to the shore, but that the medical men who visited them made a practice of returning in an hour or so and visiting their shore patients. Seymour and Ella amused themselves one day by concocting a letter, which was sent to the *Bermuda Royal Gazette*, and duly appeared the following week. They could not help laughing at the comments they heard upon it. They had written under the *nom de plume* of "Strange;" but the printer accidentally omitted the "r," and the letter appeared signed "*Stange*." Numerous were the conjectures as to who "Stange" could be; some, supposing it a classical allusion, hunted their lexicon and dictionary for its derivation and meaning. The letter was brief; but it reminded the readers that yellow fever had raged with very fatal effects throughout Bermuda in the years 1818, 1819, 1843, 1853, and 1856; 1859, notwithstanding the fever of the two last-

named periods, had been milder than its pre-
decessors, yet deaths had occurred. The letter
also called attention to the laxity of the
quarantine regulations. Seymour had almost
forgotten the letter; but it appeared to have
excited the indignation of two gentlemen who
were suspected to be interested parties; for as
they were breakfasting the Wednesday following, Ella, who was glancing through the
columns of the *Bermuda Gazette,* laughingly
observed : " You are getting yourself into a
mess, Percy; here are two assailants upon
your letter of the yellow fever."

" Indeed ! Well, I may have some fun yet.
Read them, love, and we will concert measures
of retaliation."

" To the Editor of the *Royal Gazette.*

" Bermuda, Aug. 10th, 18——.

" SIR,——

" I saw in your paper of the 6th inst., a
" letter signed " Stange," which, on account of
" the remarkable good sense and perspicuity
" displayed in it, ought not, in my estimation,
" to be passed by unnoticed, although I am

"not myself prepared to entirely coincide
"with the opinions set forth in it.   I quite
"agree with "Stange" as to the reprehen-
"sible way in which the health officers are
"permitted to go on board infected vessels,
"and then immediately return, and mix with
"the public generally, and their patients in
"particular; but he will have the kindness
"to point out how they can possibly ascertain
"the nature of the sickness on board, without
"first seeing the patient and inquiring into the
"state of the case? Unless, indeed, there be a
"medical man on board the ship, and whose
"statement, being an interested party, might
"perhaps be biassed. I have heard of a
"celebrated French quack, who (pretended
"he) could tell what his patient had had
"for dinner the day before, by looking
"down his throat; perhaps 'Stange' has
"heard of the same story, and, believing it,
"imagines the feat has only to be extended
"a little further, and carried through the
"side of the ship. I think it also a great
"pity that he should confine himself so
"entirely to a one-sided view of the ques-

" tion; and that when he states that the
" health officers of other colonial stations
" are not allowed to mix with the in-
" habitants, after having boarded an infected
" ship, he should at the same time entirely
" forget to mention the fact that they are
" an excessively well paid staff of men, and
" they have in addition to their fixed salary an
" extra allowance granted to them in event
" of their being quarantined. The convenient
" arrangement for medical men referred to
" is in a few words the following: A medi-
" cal man is expected to leave his practice,
" find his own boat, (at a cost of 10s. to
" 15s. at least, and I am now speaking
" from authority) go some two or three miles
" out to sea, in all weathers, and run the
" risk of infection or contagion our friend
" ' Stange' lays so much stress on, all for
" the fee of £2 currency—to about 26s.
" sterling; and, furthermore, to await the
" convenience and pleasure of the authorities
" for the payment of this sum. With re-
" gard to the importation or origin of yellow
" fever on this station, the question of

" its infectious or contagious character I leave
" to men of greater experience than myself
" to decide upon, and will content myself by
" asking this question : Why yellow fever
" should not originate in these islands, when
" there is not a single element wanting, either
" in temperature or humidity of atmosphere,
" that is generally believed to be the *materies*
" *morbi?* I would beg to refer your readers
" to an article in the *Edinburgh Review* for
" July, 1853, on ' Quarantine, &c.'

" I am, sir,

" Your most obedient servant,

" DASH MY WIG."

" To the Editor of the *Royal Gazette.*

" SIR,——

" In answer to the letter of your cor-
" respondent ' Stange,' I would beg to say that
" if he is aware of either of the health officers
" having performed their duty in a ' lax man-
" ' ner,' that it was as little as he could do to
" make the particular subject (if any has come
" under his notice in which either of the health

" officers have been neglectful of their duty,)
" either public, or lay the case before the
" executive, so that we may be spared the
" spread of contagion of any nature through
" their neglect ; not that I believe either of
" those gentlemen are anxious to introduce
" any contagious disease amongst us, as
" ' Stange' very unceremoniously seems to say ;
" indeed, I do not see what either of the health
" officers, excepting the one for the West End,
" has to do at all with the sick on board of a
" vessel in quarantine. The health officer for
" the West End has to attend the sick at the
" Lazaretto, and not on board the vessel.
" The sick from vessels in quarantine at St.
" George's and Grassy Bay are sent here also
" for him to attend ; and at such times he
" certainly should not be allowed to mix with
" the public. A health officer's duty I con-
" ceive is plain enough ; on going alongside
" a vessel with sickness on board he has to
" order the sick to be taken to the Lazaretto,
" and to direct this to be done by the people
" on board the vessel, and then to have the
" vessel cleansed, as soon as possible, by the

" crew.   But I would advise ' Stange' to read
" the Quarantine Act, and see if he cannot
" recommend something else than the negli-
" gence of the health officers to public notice.
" Is he aware how handsomely they are paid
" for submitting themselves to contagious
" diseases ?   How would he like to be in their
" position, to run great risk of taking the dis-
" ease they have to attend, and then receive a
" small pittance from the public, the abuse of
" the captain and crew ; the risk of being
" drowned sometimes, and of losing their
" patients on shore, at least during their
" attendance on the sick in quarantine.   Is
" this not a matter for the public, or those in
" authority to take notice of, and rectify, and
" should they permit public servants to go
" unrequited for services that are really valu-
" able to the community at large ?

· " I am, sir,

" Your obedient servant,

" HUMANITY."

" Pretty cool," said Seymour, after a pause.

"Pray do your best and send a crushing reply," said Ella.

"I have too much office work to do of my own to bother any more."

"Oh, Percy! how can you let those letters pass unanswered. Well, if you won't, I will."

"Don't you be saucy, puss," said Seymour, pulling her curls; "well, if you like to amuse yourself in my absence by scribbling, I have no objection, and I daresay your experience in writing for the "*Busy Times*" will stand you in good stead."

Seymour on his return from the office found Ella looking rather weary, surrounded by pens, ink, and paper.

"How dare you fatigue yourself in this fashion, you delicate little creature; now if you don't come out and admire the twilight, I'll cram all your papers into a portfolio and send the ink after them."

"Tyrant!" said Ella, with affected pettishness; and she and Seymour strolled into the twilight.

"Here comes Mr. Holt, Ella," exclaimed

Seymour; "he spins fine yarns about yellow fever, if one can coax him into a talking humour. Good evening, Mr. Holt," said he, as the old man approached. "Are we going to have any yellow fever this year?"

"Well I pray not, sir. It was too terrible in '43 and '53."

"You had it then?" inquired Ella.

"Indeed, ma'am, I had, and my old woman cured me, with God's help."

"How did she treat you?"

"Well, ma'am, I was put to bed, and covered over with cabbage leaves; and as they became hot the old woman put on fresh ones, and so drawed the fever out of me."

"I always thought you used mustard," said Seymour, interrupting him.

"Well, sir, some puts you—and a werry good thing it be—into a mustard bath, and covers you up with blankets, and you gets half boiled; but the fever after a while comes away."

"*You* can always tell, can you not, Mr. Holt, when the fever is in a particular place?"

" 'Deed, sir, I've smelt it more than once, and them dumb beasts, the cows, knows it likewise. I mind well seeing them one yellow fever season run out of a good spot of pasture. I thought a dog had run at them, but when I came to the place, I smelt the fever, and sniffed it back again. There was one other time that I smelt the fever; that was when I was sitting at my window, and I got up and opened the door, and the fever walked straight out of the house into the pigsty, and killed the pig."

They both laughed heartily, not only at the anecdote, but at the quaint form in which it was related; and bidding the old man good night, continued their walk.

"What a sweet little child that is," said Ella, as a little girl, the daughter of one of the sergeants, passed by.

"How fond you are of children, love."

"Yes; there are few things like a child's sympathy. I think I have read somewhere some touching lines upon it; but my own feeling is, that in good children's eyes we behold vast depth of undefiled thought.

There is so much of earnestness in all that children do, in prayer, and play—while full of love, expectation, and curiosity they seek the sympathy of their elders.   I have found too much pleasure from a good child's friendship to carelessly pass by such a pure pleasure of life.   Some persons fancy children cannot understand ; but tell them of your love for any you fear do not return it, speak to them of the charms of religion and the beauty of holiness, or unfold your grief for the loss of any one dear to you—I have ever found children do not indulge the doubt whether you deserve the love which you seek, or whether your sorrow is duly proportioned to your loss ; but though they may not gauge such matters in their thoughts, their feelings are for the time merged with yours."

"Very true, Ella ; but men are often sent forth to make their way in life at such an early age, that their attention is apt to be too much absorbed in their business to mind children."

CHAPTER VII.

UNEXPECTED DISCOVERY.

"It is the master piece of villany
To smoothe the brow, and to outface suspicion. '
HOWARD.

AT their cottage, several long and well-filled letters awaited them. There was one from Miss Ffrench to Ella, and one in a strange handwriting, with a large enclosure, for Seymour. Ella saw him looking very irate as he read, and, bending over him, pulled away the letter. " I won't let you read letters if you look so fierce," said she.

" If this does not make any one fierce, I don't know what will ; however, I don't fancy Mr. Stanley will endeavour to keep you much longer out of your ancestral estates," and Seymour read :——

" MY DEAR SIR,

"Do not burn this letter (if you look "first at the signature) without perusal. "Possibly you may remember me; if not, "Mrs. Seymour (to whom I send my most "dutiful respects) will. I sinned against "her, and, as far as possible, against you; "but another who was far more bound up in "her interests, and whom the ties of friend- "ship might have restrained, tempted *me*, and "I confess, though I now greatly and deeply "deplore it, that I lent my aid to force Mrs. "Seymour, *née* Sinclair, into the Strange "convent. But I said I was tempted. Read "the enclosed; they are genuine I pledge my "priestly word. I trust you will forgive and "forget the part I have taken in considera- "tion of the enclosed; and if you can pos- "sibly avoid it, that you will not divulge "their contents to the world.

"I remain, yours respectfully,
"FRANCIS,
"Prior of Strange Convent."

Seymour had barely done reading, when

Paymaster Fitz, and Fordbrad, who had been invited to dinner, were announced.

The usual courtesies were interchanged. Seymour observed: " I thought I had abandoned law, but I find I must rub up my former smattering ; here's a precious concern, Fitz," and he handed him a legal document.

" Who is it from ? " inquired Fitz.

" Read it out, *pro bono publico*, like a good fellow, it explains itself; " and Fitz, drawing a candle towards him, read it aloud :

"An agreement made this first day of March, 18——, between William Henry Stanley, of Strange Hall, in the county of Hampshire, of the one part, and Father Cyril Francis, of Strange Convent, in the county of Hampshire, prior of the convent of Strange, of the other part. The said William Henry Stanley hereby agrees, on or about the tenth day of June, 18——, to place his ward, Ella Sinclair, as a pupil in the Convent of Strange. And the said Father Cyril Francis, on behalf of himself and his successors, hereby agrees to pay unto the said William Henry Stanley, on fulfilment of the above condition, the sum of five thousand pounds of good British money. And it is also further agreed between the said parties, that if the said Ella Sinclair shall take the veil on or before she arrives at the age of twenty-one years no claim is to be made upon the said William Henry Stanley, his heirs, executors, or assigns, for any part or portion of the said sum of five thousand pounds, or for any interest thereon. And it is also further agreed by and between the said parties, that upon the said Ella Sinclair taking the veil, the said Father Cyril Francis, on behalf of himself and his successors, will out of the revenues of the said Convent of Strange, allow unto the said William Henry Stanley an income of four hundred pounds per annum, to be paid quarterly on the four usual quarterly days for payment, but which payment shall cease and determine on the decease of the said William Henry Stanley. It is also further agreed by and between the said parties, that should Ella Sinclair not take the veil as aforesaid, the said William Henry Stanley will repay unto the said Father Cyril Francis, or his successors, the sum of five thousand pounds, by five annual payments of one thousand pounds, such payments to commence the day after the said Ella Sinclair arrives at the age of twenty-one years, but no interest is to be charged by the said Father Cyril Francis, or his successors, on the said sum of five thousand pounds. And the said Father Cyril Francis, on behalf of himself and his successors, agrees upon the happening of the event hereinbefore mentioned, viz., the said Ella Sinclair taking the veil, will, when thereunto required by the said William Henry Stanley, execute a good and sufficient annuity deed, which shall contain such conditions, provisoes and covenants, as are usual and proper in annuity deeds. In witness thereof the said parties have subscribed their hands the day and year first above written.

WILLIAM HENRY STANLEY,
CYRIL FRANCIS,
Prior of Strange Convent.
Approved on behalf of Strange Convent,
AGATHA, Lady Abbess.
DAVID SIMKINS, } Witnesses."
PAT KELLY. }

" Well, you've had a fortunate escape Mrs.
Seymour," said Mr. Fitz. " It's very evident
that Father Francis has quarrelled with Mr.
Stanley, or cannot get the five thousand back.
It seems pretty certain it was paid."

"It is an extraordinary agreement certainly,"
said Seymour, " and Mr. Stanley was cunning
enough about it ; for I now remember that
Russell told me he suddenly went off to the
continent with Father Francis for a day or
two. See, the other deed, which is a *fac-
simile* of this, has been executed in France,
being a Roman Catholic country. I suppose
the idea was that it probably would *there* be
a binding one, and if so, *that* might make it
legal in England."

" Well, they are a pretty pair certainly,"
said Fordbrad ; " however, Father Francis
has lost his money, and I dare say Mr.
Stanley is none the better for what he got. I
suppose you won't pay it ?"

" I have not got it in the first place," said
Seymour, " and if I had ever so much I
would not give sixpence to keep the pair of
them from starving."

"For shame, Percy," said Ella. "It is not for you to wreak vengeance. It is for the all-wise God to punish them as He sees fit."

"Well, Ella, please don't speak more of them. The very thought of them makes me angry."

"You should think, dear Percy, of the good I received from them. We neither of us know how Mr. Stanley or Father Francis were tempted. Uncle was very kind to me all the time I was at Strange Hall; and Father Francis was good to me when I was a pupil in the convent; in a way, too, he saved my life, by taking me out of the vault of penitence," said Ella, shuddering. "I believe I should have died if I had stayed there."

"Ah, Mrs. Seymour, but if it had not been for him you would not have been in the convent at all," said Fordbrad.

"Now, Mr. Fordbrad, I won't have you take Captain Seymour's part. Poor Father Francis is doing all he can to repair his wrong-doing, and we must not indulge in uncharitable feelings towards him."

" Charity rejoiceth in the truth, Ella," said Seymour.

" It's very well for you to talk, sir," said she, " but as you intend using the letters he has sent you, it is hardly fair to go on abusing him."

" Never mind, Ella. Can you tell me why a hypocrite's eye, had better descry, than you, or I, on how many toes, a pussy cat goes ? "

" No, I give it up," said she, laughing. " Tell me."

" A hypocrite neat can best counterfeit, (count her feet) and so I suppose he can best count her toes," sang Percy.

" I don't see the connection, Percy," said Ella, laughing.

" I'll leave you to find out," said he, as dinner was announced.

" I heard of a pretty cool thing the other day from a Liverpool friend," said Fordbrad, as the soup was being removed, " which vies with some of your bachelor proceedings for coolness. He was always considered a pretty cool hand, Mrs. Seymour," continued he, turning to her; "I suppose you know what that means?"

"Yes, I fancy Percy has pretty well initiated me into slang."

The gentleman in question looked comical, but made no observation, and Fordbrad continued : "A clerk disappeared from one of the principal banking houses one morning; and it was soon ascertained he had taken about two thousand five hundred pounds with him. Of course detectives were set upon his track, but without avail. A few weeks afterwards he wrote to his ' chum,' enclosing fifteen hundred pounds, stating that he had been enjoying a trip through Wales, and much regretted not having been in a position to see the old cashier's face when he first ascertained the defalcation of the money."

"How very strange," his hearers remarked, " to have returned part of the money."

"Yes," replied Fordbrad; "if I had been bad enough to abstract two thousand five hundred, I should most certainly have retained the whole of it, particularly if it was in gold."

"Why in gold, in particular?" asked Ella.

"Because, Mrs. Seymour, gold is at a premium in America, whither our friend was bound."

"Well, it *was* a cool proceeding," said Seymour; "yet I have heard it equalled by an Irish beggar."

"What was that?" said Fitz.

"Merely this," he replied. "My uncle was one day walking about his grounds, when he met a beggar carrying in his hand a large key. The fellow offered to sell it for sixpence. After some bargaining it was purchased; my uncle thinking from its size it would make a good house door key. On his return he called the butler, and desired him to have the present lock removed from the back door, and a new one made which would fit the key."

"Faith, indeed, your honour," said the man, looking at it, "why it's the kay belonging to the door that you 've given me; for it was lost about a week back."

The dinner passed over; Ella retired, and the gentlemen, drawing their chairs round the open window, held converse. Fordbrad presently fell into a doze, and at length giving a long nod forward he lost his balance, falling upon Emperor, who was lying at his feet. The dog started up with a loud growl, and seized Fordbrad, but, like a good-tempered brute as he was, did not bite him; and Seymour, freeing him, they adjourned to the drawing-room, where Fordbrad confessed what he had been doing.

"He deserves well at your hands, at all events, Mr. Fordbrad; but I beg your pardon, *Captain Fordbrad* I should say, I believe."

"Yes, I have now the distinguished honour of being of the same rank as my worthy host."

"Your worthy host ought to be a major," said that gentleman, "when his responsible position is considered."

"None of your nonsense, Seymour," said Fordbrad.

"No; the first captains of Engineers, who are men of long service, and are continually placed in positions where they have to confer and transact business with colonels and generals, require rank to give weight to their opinions; and the rank of major would tend to place them more on an equal footing with their cavalry and infantry brethren than they now are. As a line officer I can conscienciously say that; and the cost would, I believe, be trifling."

"A mere bagatelle," replied Seymour. "I once went through it. I think to make all our first captains and half of the Artillery majors, would entail an annual cost of little more than four thousand pounds."

"Would you make any of the Artillery captains majors also?"

"Certainly," replied Seymour. "The responsibility of a first captain of Artillery frequently equals that of any lieutenant-colonel commanding an infantry or cavalry regiment. It certainly exceeds that of many majors. It would be a most beneficial thing for the public service; and we should see fewer young infantry majors passing over old gray-haired officers, of vast experience and service, in the Artillery and Engineers. It has been laid down, too, that a battery of artillery, with its guns, is entitled to the same honours as a regiment with its colours; surely the officers should be on an equal footing. Do you know, Fordbrad, that an aide-de-camp receives about £170 a year more than a first captain of Artillery or Engineers. I think none will say an aide-de-camp's duty, either in time of peace or war, is the most responsible or important. But be that as it may, I cannot help thinking our first captains should at least be placed upon a footing equal to that of an aide-de-camp."

" I don't see how you make out that an aide-de-camp is so much better off," said Fordbrad.

" Well,—he receives his captain's pay of twelve shillings, and staff pay of nine-and-sixpence a day. The first captain only receives eleven shillings a day pay, and a staff pay of five-and-sixpence ; no lodging or forage allowance ; * total, sixteen-and-sixpence a day. He receives also an allowance of twenty-seven pounds a year, which is totally insufficient, instead of the aide-de-camp's soldier servant ; at all events, the aide is more than nine shillings a day, or nearly £170 a year better off than the first captain of Engineers ; besides, he generally lives at his general's table."

* A few captains are by special authority granted forage.

"True, O king," said Fordbrad.

"Poor puss," said Fitz, stroking a white cat, belonging to Ella.

"Pussy, beware!" said her mistress, "he covets your eyes."

"Oh, so you've been told about the adventures we had with the cats in days of yore," said Captain Fordbrad.

"Oh, yes," she answered. "You were all very naughty."

"It's wonderful, the powers of endurance some beasts have," said Seymour. "When I was staying at Strange Hall I constantly set traps for rats, and one morning two traps had disappeared."

"Percy, don't," said Ella.

"'Tis a curious fact in natural history, my love. Well, we hunted everywhere, high and low, but could not find the traps; at length, about eight days afterwards, as I was going along one of the shrubberies, I heard a cat crying, and found one of the house cats dragging the lost trap after her. She seemed very weak and thin, but I let her out; she hobbled away, and was soon all right again. Well, at

the end of another week, in a flagged court
where food could not by any possibility have
been obtained, we found the other trap, with
a cat in it. She was caught by the paw,
and the paw held by the teeth had quite de-
cayed; but I saw her a year afterwards in
the kitchen, and though one paw was shorter
than the other, she seemed pretty happy."

Ella shuddered. "You were very cruel,
Percy, to trap the poor cats."

"The poor cats, love, should have remained
in the house, and not gone hunting for young
rabbits in the shrubberies."

"Well," said Fitz, "I can tell a tale of a
cat even more wonderful than yours, if Mrs.
Seymour will allow me."

"Relate it, please; Captain Seymour has
deadened my feelings with his dreadful
narration."

"It's merely this," said he. "I will ask
you to believe it, for it is well authenticated.
As they say, 'once upon a time' a relation of
mine had a cook; the cook owned a cat, to
which, for some reason, my relative took
a strong dislike. Returning from shooting

one day he met puss, where she had no business to be, in one of the plantations ; he fired,
and she tumbled over. Knowing, however,
that cats are tenacious of life, he fired the
second barrel at her as she lay on the ground.
He said nothing about the circumstance ; but
going into the kitchen next day found cook in
a state of wonder as to the non-appearance of
the cat. Three days subsequently he had
again occasion to descend to those regions,
where, to his horror, he saw the animal he had
shot, sitting by the fire. 'The cat has come
back then, cook,' he said. 'Yes, sir, she returned yesterday, but seems a little uneasy in
her head, which she has been scratching all
the morning.'"

"Well, that *is* a capital story," said Seymour ; "but is it really true?"

"Percy, don't be rude," said Ella. "It's not
more extraordinary than what the fox did at
Strange."

"May we hear that, Mrs. Seymour," said
Captain Fordbrad.

"Oh, certainly. One of the tenants had a
cottage built against a large bank of earth ; the

bank formed the back of the house, and one side of the roof rested upon it. Late one night a loud crash was heard, and something heavy tumbled into the house. The owner got up, and found a fox lying lifeless upon the floor. I should tell you that there were a number of fowls in a loft on the top of the house, and the fox, doubtless, had come after them. The man left him on the floor, and when he rose in the morning took him by the tail, and opening the door flung him outside; but as soon as he did that, up jumped Reynard and scampered away. The man always declares that the fox turned round and winked at him before he went off; but I for one don't believe that."

"No, I should hope not, Ella," remarked Seymour. "I don't believe half the rest either."

"Percy, for shame; you did not say so when I first told you the story."

"I believed anything in those days," said Seymour, making a droll face.

"That's just like mankind in general, I think," said Ella. "What a number of your men have medals, Captain Fordbrad!" said Ella, after a pause.

"Yes, Mrs, Seymour, they have seen a good deal of service; and medals have kept progress with the times, and are now pretty plentiful."

"Do you know when medals were first bestowed?" asked Seymour.

"I cannot say I do," he replied; "but I understand that the first medal issued to the army, was for soldiers engaged in 'forlorn hopes.' A silver medal was awarded to every officer and soldier in the 42nd Regiment for their share in the exploit of capturing a standard from Napoleon's invincible legion; and, at the suggestion of the Duke of Wellington, the army at Waterloo received a medal."

"But, Percy, how was it your colour-sergeant received a medal? He had never been in battle," said Ella.

"No, he had not; but even in time of peace the soldier can earn his medal. If he serves faithfully, and his conduct be unexceptionally correct for eighteen years in the

Artillery, Engineers, or Infantry, or for twenty-one years in the Cavalry, he may obtain a silver medal, and a gift varying from five to fifteen pounds."

" I think, Seymour," said Fordbrad, " if a man is tried by court-martial, it will be a bar to his obtaining a medal. If he is tried and acquitted, it does not, I think, count against him ; but if he is found guilty, even should the finding be held erroneous by the revising authority, and the judgment reversed, he will still be debarred from receiving a medal. And instances have come to my knowledge in which this rule has told severely. I remember well, a non-commissioned officer was tried for having made use of improper language to an officer ; but it came out in the course of trial, that he was at the time in command of a guard, and, in pursuance of his orders, interfered to prevent some friends of the officers passing into the barracks, and that the officer made use of some improper language to him. The court convicted him, and sentenced him to be reduced to the ranks, and imprisoned. The judge-advocate-general, however, reversed the finding and sentence, restored the man to his former position, and gave him all his back pay. *Mais, revenons à nos moutons.* Silver medals are occasionally bestowed upon sergeants, together with a small pension, for meritorious conduct ; and during the Crimean war, a medal and gratuity were sometimes granted for distinguished service in the field.   I fear this is hardly interesting to you, Mrs. Seymour," said Fordbrad.

"Oh, I assure you it is," said Ella. "As an officer's wife I take a lively interest in soldiers, and all that concerns them.   From what I hear, I am sure they are better off than they used to be."

"Well, certainly of late years much has been effected towards ameliorating their condition, both socially and morally," replied Fordbrad, "though their entrance into the service I fear is continually occasioned by the public-house, which I regard as the great depôt from which recruits generally are drawn.   Go into any of our large towns, especially those in the manufacturing districts, and you will generally observe gaily dressed recruiting sergeants and their satellites prowling about. By their gay uniforms, and yarns of pay, prize money, pensions, or promotion, they entice the scapegrace son, tired of home pursuits, or perchance rejected by some fickle maiden. The youth takes the enlisting shilling, and if the doctor does not reject him, he becomes a servant of the crown, and swears allegiance to her majesty."

"Well, Ella, we are to have the Prince here in a few days," said Seymour, changing the conversation.

"I am so glad to hear it," cried she, with enthusiasm. "There is so much charming scenery in these Italian-like islands, scattered as they are under the canopy of cerulean skies, that they afford ample scope to the pencil of the artist, or the camera of the photographer. I feel certain that the Prince will enjoy his stay here."

"There is a curious tradition extant about the Bermudas," observed Fordbrad. "During the American war, a convoy from England failed to find them, doubtless from their slight elevation above the sea; and the commodore returned to England, where he reported that he had sailed over the spot where they were marked down on the chart."

"Oh!" said Seymour, "Bermuda won't sink in spite of all. I went some time back to see the great globe in Leicester Square, and not seeing the Bermudas, I inquired for those islands. 'Oh! they have tumbled off,' was the answer."

The visitors shortly afterwards took leave.

CHAPTER VIII.

YELLOW FEVER.

"The heaving sighs through straighter passes blow,
And scorch the painful palate as they go;
The parch'd rough tongue nights' humid vapour draws,
And restless rolls within the clammy jaws."

ROWE.

"PERCY," said Ella, as soon as they were alone, "please revise what I have written;" and she pulled some sheets out of the portfolio.

"You go along to bed, little tease that you are; or I won't do anything."

Ella retired, treading as she went upon her cat's tail, making that quadruped yell with pain, and so startling Seymour, that he upset the little table at which he was reading. Ella alarmed at the tumult — Emperor having chimed in—ran hastily upstairs.

The next morning the letters went to the

newspaper. Ella waited with ill-disguised impatience for their publication, and intercepting the *Gazette* at the door, before her husband could prevent her, tore off the wrapper. "Now, Percy, don't they sound well?" and she read—

"To the Editor of the '*Royal Gazette.*'

"SIR,

"The facetious attack which the worthy "health officer for the East End has thought "proper to make upon my recent communi-"cation, may fairly raise him to the title of "'a bit of a wag.' The quiet manner in "which he avoids the main point, and then "endeavours to justify his conduct by quoting "the scanty remuneration he receives, re-"calls to my remembrance a tale of college "life, where the hero is suddenly inundated "by a shower of bills, and informed by his "scout, 'Shrimp,' that the 'gentlemen' who "brought them were waiting below for pay-"ment. Shrimp, however, by his master's "orders, shows them into an apartment, sets "before them sherry, and retires. The hero

" and his scout then quietly secure the door,
" and, as the Yankies say, 'make tracks '——like
" the worthy health officer, deferring the ques-
" tion at issue *sine die*. If 'Dash my
" Wig' will make inquiries of those who are
" acquainted with the quarantine regulations
" of other British colonies, he will, I think, be
" informed, that the health officers go *along-*
" *side every vessel* before she is allowed to
" come into port, and not merely to those
" hoisting a yellow flag, as in Bermuda, and
" inquire from the captain (who is bound
" under a heavy penalty to answer truly),
" from whence he is ; whether there is *any*
" *sickness* on board ; and if medical aid is
" required or not. If it is, a medical man
" (not the health officer) is sent on board, and
" should the vessel be placed in quarantine,
" so is he. By a curious chain of reasoning,
" which I confess my inability to follow, I am
" referred to the *Quarterly Review* of 1853,
" but as it does not mention this colony, I
" have the bad taste to prefer the report of
" the late commission upon yellow fever in
" Bermuda, and must remark that although

" the former report contains much valuable
" information *per se*, it can scarcely be so
" valuable for Bermuda as the latter, to which
" I refer the gallant Esculapius. I regret he
" considers my recent communication an
" attack upon him; it was not thus meant;
" but my sole object was, as I have before
" stated, to bring to the notice of those in
" authority the manner in which the health
" officers are permitted to endanger the lives
" of the inhabitants. I believe they are very
" indifferently paid; their small fee of twenty-
" six shillings is sometimes withheld for
" months, and they have occasionally to lay out
" in boat hire more than they receive; but I
" cannot admit they are ' non-conductors ' of
" fever. ' Dash my Wig's ' conclusion is
" most amusing. After stating his willing-
" ness to leave the question of origin and im-
" portation of yellow fever to wiser men, he
" attempts to show that although yellow fever
" is not at present in the islands, it certainly
" should be; like a medical man in the West
" Indies who ordered a coffin for a patient,
" who he thought was a very impudent fellow

" to recover, as he (the doctor) had to pay for
" the article, which by the way, his econo-
" mical wife turned into a press for the boots
" and shoes of the family. ' Dash my Wig's '
" ending is like the postscripts to young
" ladies letters (I hope I may be forgiven),
" which generally contain what the writers are
" most anxious to relate.

" I am, sir,

" Your obedient servant,

" STANGE.

" August 17, 18——."

" To the Editor of the ' *Royal Gazette.*'

" SIR,

" The admirable and intelligent reply
" of ' Mr. Humanity,' should not, I think,
" pass unnoticed. Like his medical compeer,
" he attempts to justify the proceedings of
" the health officers, on the score of their
" inadequate remuneration, and imputes to
" me a desire to injure them. His absurd
" quibble, ' that the health officer for the
" ' West End has to attend the sick at

" 'the Lazaretto and not on board the
" 'vessel,' (forgetting that after the said
" visit he returns to, and visits his other
" patients at Hamilton,) may fairly cause sus-
" picion that he is a 'sea lawyer;' and his
" letter is so vague, and wanders so much
" from the point at issue that I cannot think,
" although he has read my communication, he
" has understood it. I much pity the health
" officer, who as he says risks being 'drowned
" 'sometimes.' Perhaps he will state how
" *many* times he has been drowned, or write
" better grammar. Much of my reply to 'Mr.
" 'Dash my Wig' is applicable to 'Mr. Hu-
" 'manity;' the sole object of whose letters
" appears to be either to obtain a higher
" rate of pay for the health officers, or,
" failing in that laudable attempt, to justify
" their endangering the lives of the inhabi-
" tants. There may or may not be points in
" the quarantine regulations, (or rather in the
" manner they are enforced) which require
" revision, but I prefer discussing but sub-
" ject — a most important one — at a time.
" It is surely somewhat peculiar that as the

" health officers appear to be under paid, and " subject to so many difficulties and dangers, " they hold the appointments. Perchance it " is from philanthropic motives.

    " I remain, sir,

      " Your obedient servant,

        " STANGE.

" August 17, 18——."

" Well, I hope people will not bother me by replying," he observed ; " we are busy preparing for Prince Alfred's coming, and I have plenty to do without entering into a war of words in the local newspaper."

Seymour's wish was not gratified ; for a letter in a sarcastic strain appeared in the succeeding *Gazette*, requesting him to permit the name of Lindley Murray to bide in peace, and accusing him of being in want of a situation, and of seeking the post of health officer. He, however, paid no attention to these " provokes ; " and the arrival of H.R.H. Prince Alfred, with his suite, completely absorbed the attention of the Bermuda world.

VOL. III.   H

CHAPTER IX.

VISIT OF PRINCE ALFRED.

"I love the sailor; his eventful life—
    His generous spirit—his contempt of danger—
    His firmness in the gale, the wreck, and strife;—
    And tho' a wild and reckless ocean-ranger,
    God grant he make that port, when life is o'er,
    Where storms are hush'd, and billows break no more."
                                                COTTON.

AFTER pleasant days of anticipation and eager
scrutiny, the flags which signalled the approach
of vessels, or made known their numbers, at
length announced that her Majesty's ship,
St. George—upon which it was well known
His Royal Highness Prince Alfred was serv-
ing as a midshipman—was in the offing. A
few hours later she ran into Grassy Bay, the
the forts thundering a salute as she passed
by them. Then, indeed, was the public on
the tiptoe of expectation, and many and
varied were the reports circulated as to what

would be the programme in which the loyal
Bermudians would be permitted to parade
their fealty and respect to a scion of royal
blood. Let one incident suffice. It was related
that the day before his Royal Highness landed
the duty of signal-midshipman devolved upon
him, and, in the course of that duty, he answered the telegraph, " It is hoped his Royal
Highness will land to-morrow."

For a day or two after his arrival, his Royal
Highness visited, as a midshipman, at the
Admiralty and Government houses ; but on
Monday, 6th May, 1861, he made his state
entrée into the islands.

That sixth of May time will vainly endeavour to wrest from the recollection of the
inhabitants of Bermuda ; indeed, for many
previous days and weeks all classes had been
astir in an unexampled manner, exerting
themselves to render to his Royal Highness a reception which should not only
befit the occasion, but at the same time
express a loyal welcome from both rich and
poor. To aid the general rejoicings, and
co-operate with the exertions of private indi-

viduals to give *éclat* to the Prince's visit, the House of Assembly voted £700 out of the annual revenue of £15,000. About half-past one p.m., His Royal Highness with his suite, passed in the barge of the *St. George* along Hamilton Harbour, the ships dipping their flags as he advanced. They landed on a jetty specially prepared for that purpose, spread over with flags, and very tastefully adorned with Pride of India boughs, evergreens, and flowers. Every garden in the islands had contributed its quota of rare exotics to the general hoard of floral treasures. The jetty was spanned by an imposing arch, constructed of cedar and palmetto boughs, intertwined with garlands of oleander, while along its crown ran the inscription in scarlet letters, " Victoria's Noble Son !"

The most aristocratic families of Bermuda, amongst whom mingled many naval and military officers, occupied a portion of the seats along the jetty, the remainder being filled with the members of the corporation of Hamilton and St. George, and several friendly societies. His Royal Highness, who was accompanied by Major Cowell, R.E., was received by His Excellency the Governor, Colonel Harry St. George Ord, Royal Engineers, the officers commanding the garrison, and the officers commanding the Artillery and Engineers, and other distinguished personages, the band playing " God Save the Queen."

On behalf of the corporation of Hamilton, the mayor was graciously permitted to read an address, declaring the lively satisfaction which they had in being the first to welcome his Royal Highness' visit to the most ancient British colony.

A courteous reply was read by his Royal Highness, thanking the mayor and corporation for their loyal greeting, and expressing his gratification at being able to visit Bermuda.

This opening ceremony being over, his Royal Highness and suite walked along the front street of Hamilton to the public buildings. The way was thronged with a vast assemblage, of every shade of colour, from the Englishman to that of the darkest negro.

Among the crowd, marshalled under their respective emblems, were several charitable societies. The balconies and verandahs of the houses were veiled in a sea of evergreens, upon which floated rich floral accumulations ; but the lovely maidens of Bermuda, who thronged the mansions, and whose elfin hands had been unsparing in the labour of decoration, dimmed the lustre of the hour-blooming embellishments. Flags waved on every roof ; and, from the windows, mottoes and inscriptions everywhere expressed the proud delight of the multitude. But my pen would need the guidance of an old literary stager to vividly pourtray, in suffi-ciently incisive terms, the numerous forms that loyalty had adopted to express its grati-fication on this august occasion.

His Royal Highness' arrival in the public buildings was instantly made known to those outside by the hoisting of the royal standard on the roof ; and, with his suite, he soon entered the council-chamber, where his honour, John Harvey Danell, a long-tried and faithful servant of the crown, the Chief Justice of

Bermuda, and the President of Her Majesty's Council, read the following address :—

"May it please your Royal Highness,— We, the members of Her Majesty's Council in the Islands of Bermuda, beg respectfully to meet your Royal Highness with a sincere, loyal, and hearty welcome to the shores of this ancient and loyal dependency of the British Crown. It may not be in our power to give your Royal Highness that brilliant reception which has awaited you in some of the larger, more wealthy, and more populous colonies ; yet we can confidently assure your Royal Highness that the inhabitants of this little colony are not to be surpassed by any of Her Majesty's subjects, at home or abroad, in loyal attachment to our beloved Sovereign, or in personal respect for yourself, as her son, not less than as a member of that glorious profession, which, for more than three centuries, has so eminently contributed to shed lustre on the British name, and to raise to its present height the British nation. To this loyal welcome we beg to add our earnest prayer that the Divine blessing may ever attend your Royal Highness in the noble career upon which you have entered, and the high station in which your illustrious birth has placed you."

His Royal Highness read the following reply :—

" Gentlemen,—In thanking you for the kind welcome which you have given me, and for your loyal address, I do so with the same sentiments of gratitude which I have always experienced upon similar occasions. It is true that Bermuda is but a small colony; but I am well aware of the spirit of loyalty with which its inhabitants are actuated; and the reception which they have afforded me is a pleasing indication of the affection which they bear towards the Queen, and one which I shall not fail to communicate to Her Majesty. The importance of these islands to the mother-country cannot be overrated, from their geographical position and configuration; and I shall always regard them with a pecu-

liar interest, from the benefits which our navy
and commerce derive from their harbours and
resources. I thank you sincerely for your
prayers for my prosperity in my profession.
"(Signed) ALFRED.
" To the Honourable Members of Her
Majesty's Council, Bermuda."

The Speaker of the House of Assembly
then presented an address to his Royal Highness, and was honoured by a brief reply.
This over, the members of the House were
severally introduced to his Royal Highness.
The Rev. M. K. S. Frith, in the name of
the clergymen of the Church of England,
then read the following address :—

" May it please your Royal Highness,—
We, the Incumbents and other Clergy of
the Church of England in Bermuda, beg to
approach your Royal Highness with the
warmest expression of our devoted attachment
and loyalty to your august mother, our
most gracious Queen, to the Prince Consort,
and every member of the Royal Family.

We hail the happy advent of your Royal Highness to our island home with profound pleasure and satisfaction ; and, deeply sensible of the high honour you have seen fit to confer upon us by your visit, we trust, in behalf of our respective flocks, and in our own names, that you will condescend to accept at our hands a cordial and hearty welcome. May the great Head of the Church, whose way is in the sea, and whose paths are in the great waters, take you into His almighty and most gracious protection, as you go down to the sea in ships, and occupy your business thereon. May He, by whom kings reign and princes decree justice, accord to your Royal Highness a long and useful life in the service of your God and country ; and when the voyage of life is over, 'and there is no more sea, may He minister to you, and all dear to you, through Jesus Christ our Saviour, an entrance into that kingdom where all reign as kings and priests for ever."

His Royal Highness replied as follows :—

" Gentlemen,—Accept my thanks for your

loyal address, expressive of your devoted attachment to the Queen, the Prince Consort, and all the members of the Royal Family, and my sincere acknowledgments for the cordial and hearty welcome which you have given me in behalf of your respective congregations in these islands. I am happy to have this opportunity of making myself acquainted with the inhabitants of Bermuda, who have expressed themselves so affectionately towards me, and are so desirous of rendering my sojourn among them agreeable.

"   (Signed)   ALFRED.
" The Rev. M. Frith, M.A.,
        &c., &c., &c."

Before quitting the public buildings His Royal Highness held a levée, and a number of gentlemen had the distinguished honour of being presented.   He then proceeded in His Excellency's carriage to Government House, Mount Langton, passing, on quitting the public buildings, under an arch of novel and peculiar design.   Massive stone pillars formed its sides; upon them rose a superstructure of coral, brain stone, sea fans, sea rods, and other waifs of the Bermuda deep, forming the haunches of the arch; a ponderous cable, with the letter " A " moulded in a coil of rope in its centre, completing the erection. Other elegant arches lay across His Royal Highness' route, and as he emerged from the suburbs of Hamilton he was met by a merry group of juvenile tars, who heartily cheered him.

The day, however, had not been so far trenched upon as to preclude rejoicing of another character at Government House; and shortly after his return His Royal Highness was entertained at a state banquet. At its conclusion His Excellency the Governor proposed three toasts,—the Queen, the Royal Family, and His Royal Highness Prince Alfred—accompanying each with a few appropriate remarks. Need I tell of the hearty enthusiasm with which they were received. That evening the town and neighbourhood were radiantly illuminated; the placid calm of the night, the reflection of the stars,

studded over space, in the pellucid waters
of the harbour, the many coloured lights
which sparkled brilliantly, while fireworks
shot at intervals through the darkness, presented a scene which the writer of these
pages expects ever to remember.

The grounds of Government House extended to the sea on the north shore, and
Wednesday, the 8th instant, was fixed for a
regatta, in honour of the royal visit, and to
bring prominently to the notice of His Royal
Highness the admirable qualities of the world-
famed Bermuda yachts. The day was most
favourable to the larger crafts ; but the strong
S.S.W. breeze off shore was too much for
many of the little boats, and they wisely remained under shelter of the " ducking stool."

However, twelve yachts determined to
contend ; and the little squadron would have
mustered at the stake boats at the hour
named, 12·30, had not the strong wind prevented the signal gun (fired to warn all to
assemble) being heard by four of the eight
yachts that were lying to, under shelter
of the land. The other four started at

the time they had been advertised; the
Lotus at 12h. 30m. 30s.; *Eliza,* 12h. 34m.
18s.; *Pioneer,* 12h. 37m. 27s.; and *Teazer*
12h. 38m. 9s. Two other boats, the *Diamond*
and the *Nameless,* seeing what was doing,
shot down under press of canvass upon the
lee stake boat. The stewards, however,
refused to take the time of the latter boat,
alleging that she had started too late—a
curious reason. Her gallant owner, however,
under whose supervision she had been built,*
consulted his watch, and made the best of his
way along the watery course. The stewards
in the weather stake boat had no such scru-
ples, and took the time. The boats rounded
the lee and windward stake boats, the latter
being moored a quarter of a mile from the
shore, in the following manner :——

			FIRST TIME. Start.			Windward.			SECOND TIME. Lee stake boat.			Windw.		
			H.	M.	S.	H.	M.	S.	H.	M.	S.	H.	M.	S.
Lotus	-	-	12	30	30	1	15	30	1	38	30	2	20	30
Eliza	-	-	12	34	18	1	17	45	1	40	25	2	21	18
Pioneer	-	-	12	37	27	1	21	15	1	43	45	2	26	50
Teazer	-	-	12	38	9	1	22	45	1	45	30	2	28	40
Diamond	-	-	12	39	25	1	21	30	1	43	0	2	23	34
Nameless	-	-	12	41	0	1	25	20	not taken			2	32	0

* Captain Sandford, R.E.

The boats thus sailed the course :—

						H.	M.	S.
Lotus	-	-	-	-	-	1	50	0
Nameless	-	-	-	-	-	1	51	0
Diamond	-	-	-	-	-	1	43	9
Eliza	-	-	-	-	-	1	47	0
Pioneer	-	-	-	-	-	1	49	23
Teazer	-	-	-	-	-	1	50	31

The stewards, in spite of a strong protest, held that the *Nameless* had disqualified herself for the race in starting *after* the prescribed time, and the *Lotus* was adjudged the first prize, the *Eliza* the second. A little after three o'clock the yachts of the second and third classes, who were to compete, began to start for the second race. Ten started, and with the exception of the *Undine*, to which some disaster occurred on the voyage, great nautical skill was displayed. The boats of the second and third classes, as will be seen from the tables below, sailed together, the prizes, however, being allotted as if the racing had been distinct.

The 1st prize of the 2nd class was carried off by the *Nameless*, and the 2nd prize by the *Coquette*. The 1st prize of the 3rd class by the *Dolphin*, and the 2nd by the *Gladiator*.

We produce here the tables, showing the tonnage, &c., from which the time of starting was deduced; numerous experiments having verified the theory of its adaptation to the Bermuda yachts; also the time table of the boats of the second and third classes. Though items like these are more usual in a newspaper than in a three volume novel, the writer offers no apology for their introduction, knowing that several valued friends will peruse with pleasure these waifs of the past.

SECOND AND THIRD CLASSES.

	Started.			1st round to windward.			Lee stake boat.			2nd round to windward.		
	H.	M.	S.	H.	M.	S.	H.	M.	S.	H.	M.	S.
Dart - -	3	6	8	4	14	0	did not round					
Belle - -	3	10	42	did not round			do.					
Gladiator -	3	11	44	4	2	0	4	31	10	5	23	30
Dolphin -	3	15	0	4	2	39	4	30	4	5	19	30
Royal Alfred -	3	16	3	4	10	35	4	37	10	did not round		
Flirt - -	3	19	20	did not round			do.			do.		
Burchall -	3	19	20	4	9	45	4	35	10	5	24	10
Undine -	3	22	45	4	11	0	4	37	0	did not round		
Nameless -	3	23	32	4	6	15	4	31	10	5	15	25
Coquette -	3	25	17	4	8	15	4	33	50	5	19	2

	H.	M.	S.
The Nameless sailed the course in - -	1	51	53
„ Dolphin „ - -	2	4	30
„ Coquette „ - -	1	53	45

FIRST RACE.

	Teazer.		Pioneer.		Eliza.		Lotus.	
	M.	S.	M.	S.	M.	S.	M.	S.
Diamond allows or starts after -	1	16	1	58	5	7	8	55
Teazer do. -			0	42	3	51	7	39
Pioneer do. -					3	9	6	57
Eliza do. -							3	48

SECOND AND THIRD RACES.

	Nameless.		Undine.		Flirt and Burchall.		Royal Alfred.		Dolphin.		Gladiator.		Belle.		Dart.	
	M.	S.	M.	S.	M.	S.	M.	S.	M.	S.	M.	S.	M.	S.	M.	S.
Coquette allows or starts after	1	45	2	32	5	57	9	14	10	17	13	33	14	35	19	9
Nameless "			0	47	4	12	7	29	8	32	11	48	13	50	17	24
Undine "					3	25	6	42	7	45	11	1	12	8	16	37
Flirt and Burchall "							3	17	4	20	7	36	8	35	13	12
Royal Alfred "									1	3	4	19	5	31	9	55
Dolphin "											3	16	4	18	8	52
Gladiator "													1	2	5	36
Belle "																34

Boats entered for the races, their classes, owners, &c.

Boats Names.	Class.	Owners.	Distinguishing Flag.	Tonnage.
Havelock		Government	Blue, white cross	22·62
Diamond		Sir A. Milne	Red, white diamond	17·62
Teazer	1st.	Mr. Gilbert	All red	16·59
Pioneer		Mr. Tucker	All blue	15·79
Eliza		Mr. Paterson	White, blue fly	12·59
Lotus		Mr. Goeling	White, striped red	9·29
Skill		Mr. Swan	Blue, white ball	9·29
Coquette		Capt. Gammell	Pink, white	6·41
Nameless	2nd.	Lieut. Sandford	Red, black	5·66
Undine		Mr. Taylor	Square red	5·83
Flirt		Mr. Trotter	Blue, white cross	4·17
Royal Alfred		Mr. Palmer	White, blue cross	3·50
Dolphin		Mr. Swainson	All white	3·07
Gladiator	3rd.	Mr. Masson	All blue	2·50
Belle				2·23
Dart				1·60
Stella		Mr. Ralph	Blue, white star	1·13
Little Treasure		Lieut. Tisdall	Blue, white ball	1·04

During the week His Royal Highness and suite visited the light-house, erected not many years ago by Colonel Barry, R.E., and he also graced with his presence an annual school feast, given by the Rev. M. Frith to the children of his parish. Their delight at the unexpected honour was very great, and long and hearty were the cheers of the juveniles when the prince quitted the grounds.

On Friday, accompanied by his suite, he visited Walsingham, celebrated for the singularity and beauty of its caves, and for having been a favourite resort of the poet Moore. The calabash tree, under which he frequently reclined, had twined round its branches the words :—

" May fairy hands ever strew thy path with flowers."

The caves are natural, irregular hollows in the limestone rock, and from their roofs hang shining stalactites of a thousand fantastic forms. On this occasion the caves were lighted up with blue fires which reflected from the crystal walls, and in the clear waters, which flow through the caves, produced a weird and picturesque effect, and greatly gratified His Royal Highness, who, after accepting the cordial hospitality of Mr. Wood, the owner of the demesne, followed the example of most officers quartered in Bermuda, and cut some coffee sticks from the groves hard by. Then the fish ponds came in for their share of admiration, and the angel fish, blue tang, grouper, &c., peeped from their watery world at their distinguished visitor ere he departed in the *Syren* for St. George.

His Royal Highness arrived there about three P.M., and landed at the market wharf, where, as at Hamilton, a pier, festooned with all that imagination could suggest and the islands furnish, had been erected for him to land upon. Space fails me to linger upon the decorations at St. George; but I may fairly observe they should have been seen to be rightly appreciated.

The reception of His Royal Highness was most warm and loyal. Passing through the line of lovely children, who sung "God Save the Queen" as he advanced, he received and answered an address presented by the mayor (Dr. Hunter), and then he retired to Government House. A brief respite only was

allowed him, as he honoured the officers of
the 39th Regiment with his company at
dinner that evening.   Early the next—the
last day of the state visit—preparations were
made for a sham fight, the theatre of opera-
tions being the northern shore of St. George.
About ten o'clock the imaginary enemy's
fleet, consisting of the *Racer*, *Kite* (a fearful
tub) *Nettle* and *Onya*, approached the shore.
A heavy fire of blank ammunition was opened
upon them from Forts Victoria and Catherine,
and they slowly retired, returning the fire.
The boats of the fleet were now armed with
marines threatening for the fray, and under
the guns of the squadron they advanced in
two lines to the shore, and essayed to land
near the Naval Tanks.   When at 300 yards
some field guns and the rifles of the Royal
Engineers and 39th Regiment, poured in a
heavy fire, and the boats drew away.   Half-
an-hour subsequently they attempted a landing a little further to the eastward, but being
again repulsed, retreated in good order, and
rejoined the fleet which then bore up for the
dockyard.

Then Prince Alfred, the governor, admiral, and a select circle were entertained at a *déjeûner* by the officers of the Royal Artillery and Royal Engineers. The banquet was laid in a large marquee, which had been pitched in the mess garden. It had been lined with flags, and left open at both ends, which were supported by arches, one bearing the royal motto worked in white flowers on a red ground, and the other the proud motto of the Royal Artillery and Engineers *Ubique, quo fas et gloria ducant* formed in scarlet flowers on a dark blue ground. Lunch over, His Royal Highness re-embarked in the *Syren* for the *St. George*, amidst deafening cheers.

Ere his Royal Highness quitted Bermuda, he presented the Bermuda Library with an illustrated copy of "Shakespeare." The Bermuda council received at his hands three prints, from Winterhalter's celebrated portraits, of "The Queen," "The Prince Consort," and "The Prince of Wales;" and a magnificent silver challenge cup will long, we trust, be annually contested for by the yachts of the Royal Bermuda boat club.

We refrain from reviewing, in a political light, the visit of his Royal Highness to Bermuda. Whether permanent advantage will in consequence accrue to the colony, or whether the events of 1861 will pass over it as a dream, leaving but an evanescent impression, remains to be proved.

While these pages were being prepared for the press, the writer regretted to learn that, in consequence of Bermuda being a port-of-call for the Confederate steamers, the agriculture of the island is entirely neglected. Attracted by the high rate of wages offered for loading and unloading or repairing the blockade-running steamers, the labourers are incessantly engaged upon this employment. The influx to Bermuda, too, of many families from the Confederate States of America, has caused the rent of houses and the price of provisions to rise enormously. Thus, while a a few individuals — chiefly the owners of wharves—are making fortunes, the colony at large is embarrassed, and the military portion find it almost impossible to "make both ends meet."

CHAPTER X.

TRIUMPHANT RETURN.

"Thou mightiest pleasure
And greatest blessing that kind Heaven could send me!
Oh! when I look on thee, new starts of glory
Spring in my breast, and with a backward bound,
I run the race of lusty youth again." LEE.

A REPLY was at length received from Mr. Stanley, to the effect that he would make no opposition to surrendering the Strange and Rockley estates at once; it being understood that the deed of agreement between himself and Father Francis should be destroyed, and that matter hushed up.

Seymour, by the return mail, requested Captain Nott, who was yet quartered near Strange, to call in the aid of an actuary, and, as far as possible, bring Mr. Stanley's stewardship to an end. He wrote at the same time to that gentleman, to acquaint him that he acceded to his terms, and that he would

relieve him of the care, and undertake the
guardianship, of Grace Rivers, who was now
nearly nineteen.

Once more they quitted the soft Somers
Islands, never to return; and early in July
landed in England.

The day on which the young heiress entered in triumph her ancestors' lands, will
long be borne in the minds of her tenantry.

The still air and serene firmament at dawn
betokened a sunshiny day, rejoicing the hearts
of those who had laboured in love to suitably
adorn the mansion, and avenue which led to
it, in token of more than respect to their
youthful mistress, whose childish years
had been spent among them. The Roman
Catholic party spirit against Ella had died
away——for tales of her oppression had been
canvassed in all the cottages; and whatever
any malcontents might privately feel, they
were shrewd enough, at least to appear to
have forgotten the past. The woods and plantations were darkened by the vast spreading
boughs of the herculean trees; beneath
them the spider wove her cunning net, to

ensnare the gnat or fly ; the bladed soil was embroidered with the flowers of summer, smiling in clusters on the gently undulating sea of green. The turrets and battlements of the hall so vividly impressed their shapes upon the lawn, that fancy might have inclined to the belief they were planted on it. The corn-fields gently rustled and sang in the diffused light, clothing the land with a golden mantle. The deer trooped under the boughs screening the park, or strayed over the domain, while the sheep lounged lazily round their hay-cribs, or cropped the rich after-grass on the front lawn. The tender branches bent on the trees beneath the songsters that trilled their lays, and burst forth betimes in rich song. The goldfinches darted in flocks upon the thistle-down, flying through space ; the linnet and lark filled the skies ; while the sparrow chirped from her nook, and the starling whistled her accompaniment. The greater throng was seen in front of the hall ; but Ella's scholars, and those volunteers who, in days of yore, had shielded her in that eventful scene, when love strove with the convent's followers, awaited her arrival at the old lodge gate.   Over the entrance was thrown an arch of laurels, firs, and hollies, twined with rich wild roses, honeysuckle, and foxglove, a cluster of wheat ears being suspended from its crown.   In the front, "Welcome" had been worked in scarlet poppies, and the letters shone boldly out against the dark green ground.

The ancient moss-clad lodge was festooned with garlands of evergreens and wild flowers, and bees were murmuring around them, and gathering in a rich store.

At length the carriage approached.   The band of the volunteers played the first bars of "Home, sweet Home;" and while the horses were removed from the carriage by many eager to assume their place, the scholars sweetly sang some verses specially composed for the happy occasion.

I.

"She wore a wreath of roses,
The night that first they met;
Her lovely face then smiled
Tho' her curls were not of jet.

Her footsteps had the lightness,
Her voice the joyous tone,
The tokens of her trusting heart
Where sorrow was unknown.
We saw her in those happy days,
Indeed we see her now;
But without the wreath of roses,
Upon her snowy brow.

II.

" A wreath of orange blossoms,
That now we meet she wears,
The expression of her features,
Bears no trace of earthly cares.
For standing by her side is *one*,
Who strove, and not in vain,
Who came in haste from distant lands,
His English bride to claim.
She's long been absent from us,
Thank God! we see her now,
With the wreath of orange blossoms,
Upon her snowy brow.

III.

" Long may we all behold that brow,
May health its garland wreathe,
Around her and the warrior youth,
Who now his sword may sheathe.
She'll weep no more in solitude,
For there's a loved one near,
To press her hand within his own,
To wipe away her tear.
Long may they remain among us,
And long may they reign over us
In the pride of youth and beauty
God save our youthful queen."

Ella was dressed in a flowing white muslin, trimmed with blue silk, over which a China shawl was thrown. She had, in honour to her almost regal reception, put on the wreath of orange blossoms which she had worn at her ocean bridal, and repeatedly bowed her acknowledgments, as the carriage was drawn by the volunteers to the Hall, amidst the cheers of the tenantry.

"I won't bow, my own," said Seymour; "it's all for you; and I enjoy too greatly seeing all your honours to take part in them."

They alighted at the door, and Grace Rivers, who still wore mourning, rushed down the steps into Ella's arms.

"My lovely pet!" Ella murmured. "Are you here all alone?"

"All alone," said Grace. "Mr. Stanley went away yesterday. I've been very good; and when Captain Nott called, sent him word 'that Miss Rivers did not receive company in the absence of her guardian.'"

Ella looked into her laughing eyes. "Never mind, Gracie, we'll ask him to come *now*. I don't mean to tease you," said Ella, as she noticed her crimsoning; "but I can't help it to-day;" and she drew a piece of scarlet ribbon from her pocket, and held it against Miss Rivers' face. " I don't know which is the deepest crimson, you naughty girl; we shall have to look very closely after you, I can see."

"Don't Ella," said Grace. "Come and see my arrangements, and look after your tenants, not after me."

The cousins, accompanied by Captain Seymour, passed over the grounds, Ella receiving at every step the hearty congratulations of her dependants. Ample cheer had been provided for old and young; Punch and Judy enlivened the gay scene; and donkeys had been provided for the school children to ride upon in turns. These animals were intended to canter or trot a certain distance and back again; but they soon discovered what was required; and, perhaps, indignant at the one-sided arrangement, whenever they had completed half their course, they stopped short, lowered their heads, and over went the children—the donkeys quietly trotting back, minus their burden.

Ella found time to glance hastily at her girlish haunts. She fancied her favourite trees were about to change their leaves from green to yellow; but flowers were still plentiful and gorgeous, and the blossom of the hawthorn were fading away in their ripeness. All around seemed " to shout for joy and to sing." The day, as it advanced, became chilly; and Ella, warned by seeing the white fog rising from the stream and spreading its thin stratum across the land, returned with her companions to the spot where rustic revels were in force.

Her re-appearance was the signal for reiterated cheering; and Ella, resting on her husband's arm, said a few never-forgotten words to her tenantry, and then retired to the Hall, leaving them to their mirth, which was prolonged far into the night.

CHAPTER XI.

CONVERSATION.

" But conversation, choose what theme we may,
And chiefly when religion leads the way,
Should flow like waters after summer show'rs,
Not as if raised by mere mechanic powers."
                                    COWPER.

LIFE passed gently to our heroine; but yet a
thorn mingled in the garland of happiness
which encircled her—Grace Rivers was still
a Roman Catholic.   Ella and Seymour could,
if they had so chosen, have prevented her
attendance at the ceremonies of her religion;
but they did not consider it right to do so at
her age, and Grace was, accordingly, permitted
to indulge the bent of her inclinations.   Her
friends, whenever opportunity offered, pointed
out the bright, glorious truths of the gospel,
undimmed by the obscurity of the traditions
interwoven by the Church of Rome.

"Ella," said Grace, one day, "do you
believe that Roman Catholics cannot or will
not be saved?"

"I could not dare to think so, Grace. It
is not for human beings to limit the mercy of
God. We are told, too, that 'if any man
build upon a true foundation,' which is Jesus
Christ, 'his work shall be made manifest,
and if it abide he shall receive a reward.'
There are many Roman Catholics perhaps
in England, certainly in Ireland, who have
never heard the message of our Saviour—'I
am the way, the truth, and the life,' and,
'none can come to the Father but through
me;' but I would ask you earnestly to consider whether you have not had advantages of
instruction, and opportunities of reading the
Bible without molestation, which they have
not had, and to think upon our Saviour's own
words: 'To whom much is given from him
will much be required.'"

Strange as it may appear to the reader,
Father Francis was one of Ella's earliest
visitors. He had asked permission to call,
and Ella cheerfully accorded it. She bore him

no malice for what he had done, or rather
endeavoured to do, to her; and the priest
during her absence, in a season of distress
amongst the tenants, had laboured in a most
exemplary manner to relieve and make known
their wants, and collect money, fuel, and other
necessaries for them, quite irrespective of
the religion of the recipients. Father Francis was anxious that Grace Rivers should
enter the convent, but this Ella steadily
opposed. "If at her age she chooses to
attend your chapel, and participate in the or-
dinances of your religion, father, my husband
and I will not prevent it; but I trust you will
remember her constitution is very delicate,
and it would not be safe for her to fast; indeed,
I should not permit it, after what her doctor
told me. As to her entering the convent
with that lady abbess who behaved so cruelly
to me, I will not for an instant entertain such
a proposition."

"The abbess you speak of has quitted,"
replied Father Francis, "she was called to
duties elsewhere. The lady who now presides
over the nuns is all that we can desire.

Perhaps you will not object to visiting our nunnery, Mrs. Seymour ? "

" If Captain Seymour will go with me, I shall be very glad to do so," replied Ella. " But why did the abbess leave ? I suppose she was too cruel."

" I hope you will not press . me to answer," replied Father Francis, in a most courteous tone.

" Certainly not," and Ella smiled ; " but I can draw my own conclusions," she thought. " Have you many poor dependent on the convent now ? "

" The times are getting better, God be praised. No, there are no cases at present that we have not funds to meet," replied Father Francis.

" Well," said Ella, " if you require money or employment for your parish, I will always endeavour to help you."

" I thank you, Mrs. Seymour," said Father Francis, rising. " Would that there were more like you, ready to help the poor, irrespective of their religion ! Much of the antagonistic feeling between Protestants and Roman Catholics

would be dispelled, in Ireland particularly—"
and Father Francis bowed himself out.

Captain Nott was presently announced, and
he and Seymour began to talk over the affairs
of the nation at large ; then changing the subject to those of the British soldier—

" I suppose we shall agree in the main,"
said Nott, "and probably retain our own
opinions ; but I confess I like to see that in one
grand point at least the soldier has been kept
up with the times."

" How do you mean ?" asked Seymour.

" I mean this," said Nott : "any man in
past days enlisting in our own corps, the
Royal Engineers, discovered when the last
step had been taken, that though the enticing
placard, which had acquainted him that a few
young men of good character, especially those of
every trade under the sun, were required to
serve in the royal corps, the bounty which it
promised him was a visionary humbug ; as his
kit, which he was compelled both to receive and
to pay for, not only swallowed up the bounty
but obliged him to commence his martial
career heavily in debt.   I am glad to say that

has been altered. I have heard some old fogies grumble at the supply of comfortable flannel shirts and gloves free of charge to soldiers. I always feel strongly tempted to ask what they wear themselves, and to tell them that when they have a good article, to wit a soldier, they had better take care of it, as, even in a pecuniary sense, it pays to do so. In past days, the same uniform was deemed suitable whether a soldier was bound for India or Canada; but our enlightened understandings of this epoch comprehend that the soldier is a man of flesh and blood ; and while long boots, fur coats, and warm clothing are very comfortable in Canada, white trousers, loose coats, and white caps are the thing for India."

" There has been but little change in a soldier's pay for many years," observed Seymour, " but whatever there has been is for the better——I confess I am surprised that a system which creates an amount of trouble, and is very expensive, should still be in force——I mean paying a soldier, say, a shilling and twopence a day, and then deducting a few pence for his daily allowance of bread and meat. However, it's an ill wind that blows no one good : and I am certain if a soldier received his rations free of charge, and was not called upon to pay eightpence or nine-pence a day for his washing, messing, and rations when in health, or tenpence a day for his maintenance in hospital, a good many clerks who puzzle about these little et ceteras would be sent about their business. So, perhaps, it's as well that the old coach should jog on as in times of old."

" Well, I don't like to growl," said Nott ; " I've had much to be thankful for ; but I confess, if I pity one class of men more than another, it is the lance-corporals in the Royal Engineers. A man promoted to that rank not only receives no additional pay, but actually is out of pocket. As a private soldier he re-ceives, as you are aware, for his labour on the works a shilling a day ; but when he is a lance-corporal the duties of his rank occupy so much of his time, that he is not able to work so often, and consequently he forfeits, or rather does not receive, his shilling. Indeed I have known the rank refused by several, as they considered themselves better off as private soldiers; and others who were lance-corporals commit trivial offences to lose it. If two-pence or threepence a day were added to the lance-corporal's pay, a very deserving lot of men would not be paid a farthing too much; greater contentment would ensue; and the cost would be a mere bagatelle—a few hundreds annually.

CHAPTER XII.

CHRISTMAS AT STRANGE.

"The holly gleams in yule log's light,
The mistletoe bough is hung
In ev'ry city great and small,
And Christmas chimes are rung."

THE AUTHOR.

THE Christmas that year at Strange Hall was, by mutual consent, a quiet one; for Grace Rivers' nineteenth birthday was past, and she had made Ella and Percy aware of her fixed resolution to enter Strange Convent. Her guardians mourned over her determination, and the more so as she had unintentionally saddened the heart of a valued friend who had long loved her for her goodness, and for herself *alone*, undeterred by what the world would think when the gay fascinating Captain Nott, the hero of many a pleasure party, and a general favourite with the fair sex, wedded

a portionless girl.   Nott had endeavoured to
obtain a private interview with the young lady,
but she had fathomed his intentions, and
desirous of sparing him, positively declined to
accede to his request.

But Nott was not to be baulked, as he con-
fided to Ella, "by a young lady's whim," and
taking his leave for that day invited himself to
dinner the next; and horrified Grace, and
completely took his friends aback, by making
her a proposal of marriage before them, after
the servants had left the room.

Ella and Seymour kindly retired, and Nott
was left to plead his own cause.   Their interview was long and distressing to both ; for
Grace said what Nott construed into an ac-
ceptance of his offer.

The young lady, bewildered at what she
had done, at length told him "if he would
turn Roman Catholic she would be his bride."

A bitter struggle took place in the young
man's heart ; but he remembered that it did
not "profit a man to gain the whole world,
and to lose his own soul."   In clear mournful
accents, which often recurred forcibly to Miss

Rivers, he replied, " I love you above all in this world, but I do not love you more than my Saviour. He has declared that " him that denies Him before men, will He also deny before His father in heaven.' I am convinced the Roman Catholic religion is in many points opposed to the pure inspired word of the Most High. I dare not leave my hold on everlasting happiness for an earthly love." He hastily turned away, but turned again. " I do not mean to be unkind," he said— " Farewell, God help you." Nott passed out into the darkness, wishing he might be ordered to wander he cared not whither, and gain the opportunity of stifling his sorrow amid the thickest of martial strife, or in some of the most responsible duties of his profession.

Over Grace Rivers' feelings we draw a veil; but, perhaps, from that hour Nott was dearer to her than he had previously been.

A gifted authoress makes her hero tell us, " The love of gambling is more intense than was ever the love for woman." Her reasoning is familiar to those who have perused the

" Morals of Mayfair." Yet we cannot admit her inferences here. Men (and women too) will toil and undergo vast hardships in the pursuit of wealth ; but glance, if you are permitted, into the hidden recesses of thought, which in the breast of many a man of the world, wedded to its pursuits and amusements, lie buried deeply——so deeply that he may not be aware of its existence. He will tell you, though he may have drunk of the cup of infamy, of the sparkling waters, of the fading joys of time ; though vice may fling her heavy chain around him, and though he may sneer at religion, yet for all *that*, a more intense, a more enduring love than the desire of riches has burned at some time within him——some one in waking or in sleeping hours he has seen, for whom he would go to greater lengths, for whose sake, for whose love, he would undergo what 'he would not, were gold *alone* to be his reward.

Or glance at one of another stamp, who appreciates riches for the good they would enable him to do, but also is not unmindful of the comforts and luxuries they would be the means of bestowing upon himself and those he loves. He may toil on for riches, he may desire them for the reasons I have mentioned; but will that man sell his love to one whose worldly possessions are her chief adornment, who knows of the pearl of great price only in sound? I trow not. Appreciating the value of money, the comforts and the influence it will bring him, he will never labour for wealth as he will do to win a true woman, one who would be a helpmate, true and kind, against whose love time might surge, as storms assail the rays of sun or stars——in vain.

God help him if he be deceived in the heart of her he has sought; may she not prove to love the gaieties of the world better than the duties of her home. We will give another case; of those whose homes are unhappy; who seek to leave them early in life. The world will say many an unkind thing of them——of a girl especially——whose desire is often thinly veiled; but place wealth in her grasp, she will tell you there is a joy she cannot taste in her father's home; but she waits patiently to

surrender her trusting heart to one who promises, at least, to give her the happiness she
longs and prays for; and she thinks not, it
matters not to her, whether he be rich or
poor, so long as he will only love her.
Again — an orphan girl has given her love
to one whose heart is a re-echo of her own,
and a guardian, who does not wish her to wed
the object of her choice, treats her with
harshness, perhaps ventures upon cruelty.
We should be sorry to suppose that the greed
of gain could ever produce that burning desire
for revenge, (restrained probably by the dread
of the law) that would fasten on the mind of
the lover when he realised that she who had
promised to become his most prized earthly
treasure, and whose life had been dimmed by
the loss of her parents, had for his sake been
persecuted or ill-treated by a *legal*, but not a
natural protector.

Ella persuaded Seymour to go with her
over the convent, and see all that they would
shew them. The lady abbess received
them, and took them into her own apartment.
Her history was a sad one. She had been

wedded to one to whom for years she had
been attached; but cruel reports of false
dealings, foolishly credited by her, had kept
them apart, until one day, under perhaps
romantic circumstances, they met, when their
doubt and fears were dispelled by mutual
explanations.

Yet her married life had been fearfully
shortened; on the threshold of the church,
as they were returning from the ceremony,
her husband felt faint, and in a few hours
was lifeless.

Her gentle, yet sorrowfully dignified de-
meanour, struck both Ella and Seymour.
She wore the dress of her order. A long
robe of coarse serge reached to her feet.
She was girt with a leathern band, from
which her rosary was suspended. The remains of her luxuriant hair were indistinctly
visible beneath the white bandage which
encircled her forehead, and the black veil
hung in heavy folds from her head. Her
sombre simple garb seemed to lend to her
beauty a grace that art would have failed to
produce. She told her visitors she had now

for many years been a nun; she had no
hopes or sympathies with the out-door world;
she enjoyed the calm retreat of the convent
walls too greatly to harbour a desire beyond
them.

Yet they could not pity her as she passed
with queen-like grace through her dominions;
pointing out as she went everything of beauty
or interest.   Paintings, and sculpture on
Scriptural subjects beautified the chapel and
school-rooms.   The latter contained a piano-
forte and harp.   The drawing-room was
elegantly furnished, and its walls hung with
rare paintings and engravings.

The shrines of the sisterhood forcibly re-
called the days of the past to Ella, as they
stood in their simplicity decorated with the
best flowers that the season of the year would
produce.

The lady abbess took them through a well-
selected library—in which Ella as a pupil had
formerly been permitted to sit—enriched with
books and foreign curiosities, the gifts of
wealthy Roman Catholic visitors.

After they had inspected this, the lady

abbess sweetly remarked, " I have nothing more that you will care to see."

" There is one spot I should like to visit. I know it of old," said Ella, timidly.

" You may," said the abbess, calmly ; and she led the way to their last earthly home. The little city of the dead was surrounded with cypress, fern and willow trees, which darkly drooped over the plain wooden crosses which marked the grave of those sisters who had departed hence.

" Here is a spot, Mrs. Seymour," she remarked, " where the controversies of religion may be hushed, and we can gaze upon the mounds marking the spots where rest the remains of those who are gone, with patient resignation, and draw from them a lesson of meditation."

They soon after took their leave, but Ella did not easily forget the peculiarly interesting abbess.

" She would be kind to Grace I am sure," she said to Seymour on their return.

" She might, or might not," replied Seymour. " I have seen so much of the effects of placing absolute power in the hands of one person, that I greatly abhor the practice ;—and if Grace is wise she will keep out of her clutches ;—besides, even with the most kindly intentions, I presume the abbess has to adhere to certain rules."

" But what did she take you aside, in that mysterious manner for, Ella, when I was looking at the drawing-room ornaments ? "

" Well, she rather surprised me, certainly," replied Ella ; "but she told me that as there was only one vacation in the year, and as some of the pupils stayed on all the time, she was sometimes at her wits' ends to amuse the dear girls, and wanted to know if I could give her the names of any new plays, as they sometimes had private theatricals.

" Nonsense," replied Seymour, " what *did* you say ? "

" I told her I went very little into the gay world, so hardly knew what went on there ; and that I never entered a theatre, so could not help her in the way she wished."

" Was she sorry ? "

" Well, she seemed rather surprised that

we never went to the theatre," and said she hoped " we should not have a bad opinion of her ;" and then she took me into the room they used for the rehearsals. There was a screen across one corner, and after we had been some little time looking at the dresses and other things, some one peeped from behind it, and the abbess made the young lady come out; and, lo, a very pretty girl, with long glossy black curls, but dressed in *knickerbockers*, appeared. Evidently she had just dressed for some theatrical performance.

" Well, Ella, we live and learn, certainly," replied Seymour. " My opinion of the abbess is raised ; but here we are at our country home. When are we to have the pic-nic to Place House ?"

" Percy," said Ella, earnestly, " I don't want a pic-nic to Place House, I have a strong fancy that a pic-nic *there* would end with something dreadful.

" Why, Ella, what on earth has happened ? "

" Nothing," replied she, " but I cannot help the feeling."

Seymour tried persuasion, ridicule, and argument, all in vain; Ella had got the notion—or whatever our readers may call it—too firmly into her mind, to be coaxed or argued out of it, and would not be pacified until he said, "Very well, we will do as you like about it."

"What silly trash," muttered he, when he was left alone. "I will try some day, however, to get her to go, if only to prevent her indulging such an extraordinary fancy with regard to any other place."

CHAPTER XIII.

STRIFE.

And she forgot the stars, the moon and sun,
And she forgot the blue above the trees,
And she forgot the dells where waters run,
And she forgot the chilly autumn breeze,
She had no knowledge when the day was done,
And the new moon she saw not ; but in peace
Hung over her sweet Grace evermore,
And moistened her with tears.

Altered from KEATS.

" ELLA," said Grace, with a mournful smile, the day after Christmas day, " I want to do what you were not permitted to do——to walk round the domain for the last time. Please come with me."

" Grace, Grace, why will you break our hearts, love? Oh, stop while you can, my sweet cousin," said Ella, throwing her arms round her neck, and weeping bitterly.

" No, Ella, no. Something tells me I should enter on my noviciate at once. Pray do not

L 2

refer to it again. Let not our last hours be those of gloom."

They wrapped themselves in warm cloaks, and quitting the cheerful fire blazing in the drawing-room, sallied out, and passed into the old garden. King winter reigned sole monarch. The beech trees, Ella's old favourites, moaned and tossed their ponderous branches, as if they, too, were troubled, and knew Grace Rivers would no more walk beneath them. The blast blew keenly, and the few leaves that still clung upon the trees were rapidly falling, and they looked desolate and bare. The underwood of laurels, and the golden and hedgehog hollies relieved the bleak scene, and the coral berries of those handsome shrubs—which have so frequently figured in poetry—were dotted over them in vast profusion.

" Such is life, Ella," said Grace, stopping opposite the old ruin. " True, indeed, are the prophet's words, 'we all do fade as a leaf.' I see it forcibly *now*. In the spring time when all is bright, joyous, and beautiful the young buds and leaves come forth ; in the summer they attain maturity; in the autumn they fall, dropping off by degrees, leaving at length the trees in winter time leafless and bare. Our lot is, indeed, like the leaf. We first enter this world in the helpless state of infancy; in a few years we attain to womanhood, with many (as with you, love,) a season of pride—of joy; after the lapse of another period we sink into the autumn of life; and, finally, the winter of the grave closes the scene."

"Yes, my own Grace, and you may carry your simile further; as in the spring the buds and leaves burst forth in renewed splendour, so there is a bright glorious hope to the Christian beyond the winter of the grave. A kingdom filled with mansions prepared by our Saviour himself; and not, dearest, through the intercession of any saint or angel, or even by the mediation of the Blessed Virgin."

"Hush, Ella," said Grace, "I cannot bear it."

"You have infected me with the spirit of description, Grace," said Ella, after a pause.

" What better subject than that text you have
quoted, ' We all do fade as a leaf.' "

" Well, improvisatrice, proceed"——and, leaning against one of the giant trees, Ella chanted
in subdued accents :——

I.
" These words that in Isaiahs days,
      Were spoken for mankind,
   Apply to us in later times,
      Should thro' our thoughts be twin'd.

II.
" They point to us, how nature's God,
      Our lot has allied here,
   With trees and leaves, those fragile things,
      That we this name may fear.

III.
" How in the spring time's joyous days,
      Lessons of love they teach,
   The young, like leaves, are bright and fair,
      Ere manhood's years they reach.

IV.
" As in the summer's mellow days,
      The leaves still glisten bright,
   So manhood's days have blessings, oft
      Mingled with gloom of night.

V.
" Then in the autumn's fading leaves,
      Which quickly strew the ground,
   There lies an emblem of the old,
      Ending their long years' round.

VI.

" As a dark cloud o'ercasts the light,
    Of radiant summer day,
  Or as the morning dews from earth,
    Vanish and pass away.

VII.

" And as in spring, and summer, too,
    Stray leaves will strew the ground,
  So young and fair, are snatch'd away,
    Their place is no more found.

VIII.

" The young and those in prime of life,
    Oft are cut quickly down,
  Their bodies to the earth return,
    Whence first they had their form.

IX.

" Their spirits go to God, from whom,
    At his command they came,
  Eternal life or endless woe,
    Awaits them—bliss or shame.

X.

" And as at close of wintry days,
    The leaves in splendour fresh
  Burst forth, and clothe the barren trees,
    There is a state past death.

XI.

" Beyond the winter of the grave,
    Lies a golden city bright,
  Whose fruit blooms ever, and whose leaves,
    Will set the nations right.

XII.

"The shining blessed there pour forth,
    Angelic songs of praise,
To Him who sits upon the throne,
    And new songs to Him raise.

XIII.

"For by the death and blood of Christ
    Alone, they share that light,
Brighter than sun, or stars, or moon,
    That day uncheck'd by night.

XIV.

"There is another state, wherein
    The devil reigns for ever,
But 'twixt them lies a blacken'd gulf,
    That none can pass or sever." *

"Is that your own, Ella?"

"Yes, I composed it; partly as I stood here, partly as I went on. I used, when in Italy, to hear Italian ladies improvise."

"I cannot understand you, dearest girl," said Grace, with an effort to appear cheerful.

The sun was now at the horizon: all day clouds had shut out his light, now they—

"Driven before the gale,
    Hurry thro' the sky,
The darkness retiring rolls over the vale,
And the stars in their beauty shine forth on high."

* From original unpublished MSS.

Clear red rays, as of burnished gold, beamed forth, tracing a golden pathway upon the snowy pall which overspread the fields beyond them. Still they stood and mused. They peeped over the boundary wall, to the foot of which the flood tide had risen, and witnessed a sinuous shoal of wild fowl returning to their nightly lair amongst the rushes. Their wings glistened in the glory of the setting sun, as scintillating meteors which appear for a few instants, and then vanish.

Grace turned away with a plaintive sigh, followed by Ella.

The distant bleating of the sheep rang cheerfully through the old garden, while the echo gave back the distant baying of Mr. Langton's blood-hound. Two rabbits bounded across their path, and at a word from Ella Emperor gave chase, crushing through the dead branches and brushwood, and was at once lost to sight in the irregularities of the ground, and the now waning light.

" Farewell, loved scene," said Grace, turning as she reached the gate.

" Come in now," said Ella.

" Not yet," said she, softly ; " I want to
see the long walk.   I can bear all."

They entered.   Even winter had hardly
injured the green aspect ; for the laurels, box,
hollies, and evergreen oaks flourished right
well, though the trees looked barren enough.
The twilight closed upon them, and the
shades of evening fell fast ; a cold north wind
had set in, and Ella was not sorry when
Grace said, with a deep drawn sigh, " I am
ready now."   In silence they returned.   Seymour was in the drawing-room ; he would
have spoken, but a sign from Ella kept him
silent.

" Grace," said Ella, shortly after the re-
luctant consent had been wrung from Seymour, " I am going to take advantage of the
favour we have granted you, and beg you to
listen to what I shall say : you know well
enough if it had not been for Percy I should
not have been here.   I know not where I
should have been.   Why does the Church of
Rome deny the wine in the Holy Communion
to the laity ?   In the four gospels, (look at
your Douay Bible and see if I am not correct)

wherein we have given the account of the Last Supper, did our Saviour deny the cup to his disciples ? "

" It does not follow, Ella," replied Grace, " that because *all* the apostles drank of the cup, that *all* the faithful are commanded to do so, any more than all are commanded to consecrate, or to administer the Holy Sacrament."

" Grace, no distinction between the bread and wine was made by Christ ; why should *men* make a difference ? The apostles were commanded ' to go unto all the world, and to teach all to observe whatsoever He had commanded them.' He has commanded us, ' this do in remembrance of me,' that is, receive the Holy Sacrament. In another place Christ has said, ' Except ye eat the flesh of the Son of man *and drink his blood*, ye shall not have life in you.' "*

Grace made no answer, and the conversation ended.

* St. John vi., 54 (Douay version).

CHAPTER XIV.

GRACE RIVERS BECOMES A NOVICE.

" So young—too young—consigned to cloistral shade,
Untimely wedded—wedded, yet a maid!
And hast thou left no thought, no wish behind,
No sweet employment for the wandering mind—
Thou wert immured, poor maiden—as I guess,
In the blank childhood of thy simpleness;
Too young to doubt, too pure to be ashamed,
Thou gavest to God—what God had never claimed."

COLERIDGE.

YET again was the chapel at Strange the scene of a solemn ceremony. Despite Ella's and Seymour's entreaties, Grace persisted in her resolution to take the veil. Seymour did not think it right to prevent her; for though not yet of age, he considered she had better be at liberty to act for herself. She entreated Ella to support her to the altar. " It is the last request I shall make of you in this world," said she, mournfully, when Seymour hesitated.   And they consented.

Father Francis had for a time left England, his place being supplied by an amiable good-natured man.

The church and avenue were thronged as in Ella's day, and many a tear was shed, and many words spoken in pity, as the orphan, but not friendless girl, arrayed in bridal dress, a wreath of orange blossoms encircling her brow, passed on amidst the crowd, who had been soothed and cheered in hours of suffering by her kindly speech and appropriate gifts.   All, however, knew the act was her own desire, and the utmost order prevailed.   Leaning on Ella's arm, she advanced to the altar, Seymour standing behind her; and an address was delivered by a Carthusian monk, very similar to what Ella had been compelled to hear.   The same prayers were read, and once more did the archbishop's voice thrill the congregation as he pronounced the vows Grace Rivers was to take.   She did not, as Ella had done, call wildly for aid, but in a trembling voice, kneeling before the altar,

at the feet of the archbishop, she solemnly
(as the mistaken girl believed) abjured the
world. The abbess advanced; she removed
the wreath that encircled Grace Rivers' fair
hair. A distant chant of the appropriate
anthem was heard, and the archbishop standing at the altar, blessed the habit she was to
be attired in, in these remarkable words:
" Oh, God, most faithful promiser, and never
failing bestower of everlasting benefits, who
hast promised thy faithful the garment of
salvation, and the raiment of endless bliss, we
humbly implore thy clemency that thou
wouldst bless these garments, the emblems of
lowliness of heart, and of contempt of the
world, by which thy servant is visibly instructed of her holy intention; that under
thy protection she may preserve the habit of
holy chastity, which through thy inspiration
she has received, and be clothed with a happy
immortality, as she is now dressed temporally
in the garb of thy sacred promise, through
our Lord Jesus Christ, thy Son, who liveth
and reigneth one God, world without end.
Amen."

As Sister Grace appeared in her novice dress, the choir were chanting :—" Who is she that cometh up from the desert, flowing with delights, leaning upon her beloved ? Thou art all fair, my beloved, meek, and beautiful. Come, my spouse, from Libanus ; come from Libanus ; come, thou shalt be crowned."

Other prayers followed ; at length Grace, who was on her knees, was directed to rise, and the archbishop, putting on his mitre, which he had a few minutes before laid aside, handed her the cinture, which she presented to the abbess. This lady then fastened it round Sister Grace, and the archbishop holding the white veil over her, the crowning point of the ceremony was completed as it was placed on her head with this speech :— " Receive the white veil, the emblem of inward purity, that thou mayest follow the Lamb without spot, and mayest walk with Him in white, in the name of the Father, and of the Son, and of the Holy Ghost. Amen."

The abbess invested her with the cloak of the Church, the archbishop saying : " May the Lord restore to thee the robe of immortality, which thou didst lose in the prevarication of thy first parent, in the name of the Father, and of the Holy Ghost." "The Lord be with you," he added, extending his hands over her, "and henceforth relinquish your worldly position and name," said he, solemnly, "and you who art in the world called Grace Rivers, shall henceforth, *nella religione*, be named Sister Grace."

Ella, whose slight form shook beneath her grief, tearfully clung to her, and Grace Rivers, who was now weeping, passed into her living tomb.

In a few moments a panel behind the high altar opened, and she again appeared. Her hair had been severed from her head, and the white coif and noviciate veil had, as we have seen, been substituted for the bridal array she had previously worn; but soon she was conducted before the altar, and lay prostrate, the choir chanting the hymn, "Veni Creator." The prayer that followed being ended, Sister Grace was plentifully besprinkled with holy water, and making a genuflexion to the Holy

Sacrament, she knelt before the abbess, who tenderly embraced her. She then went round to each of the sisters of the order that were present, embracing, and being embraced by them.

Other prayers completed the ceremony. Grace, when all was over, appeared at the postern-gate of the convent, and received the applause and compliments of her Roman Catholic friends and acquaintances, and the sympathy and pity of her Protestant ones. Even strangers were allowed to speak to her, and were expected to pay compliments to the falsely called spouse of Heaven.

She soon, however, withdrew into the convent, and Ella and Percy mournfully returned to the Hall.

Nott came there more than ever after Sister Grace had entered the convent, and his distress of mind was very painful to Seymour and Ella.

" Are you going to the Goodwood ? " said Ella, late one evening, endeavouring to divert the current of his thoughts, which were evidently far away with Sister Grace.

"No," replied he; "I was there once, and was rather disappointed with the racing—I mean in not seeing the horses all the way round the course."

"Well, I rather agree with you," said Seymour. "I was very much pleased with the Chester races, which I was at last year. There you have a capital view, either from the grand stand, the bridge, or the opposite side of the river."

"The course is very small, is it not?" inquired Ella.

"I think it is about a mile round, but _____"

Their conversation was interrupted by a knock at the door, and the butler entered, gun in hand, breathless, and deadly pale.

"What's the matter now?" said Seymour. "Speak, man, can't you? and what are you doing with the gun?"

"Oh, sir, I didn't mean to do no harm, sir," said he, at length; "but I went down to the river to try for some of the ducks, and as I was a hiding among the bushes, up jumped something, and I let fly, and, Oh, sir, it was not a duck at all, but the Alderney cows calf ! ” *·

This was too much for the gravity of the party, and the Hall resounded with peals of laughter.

“ I feel that laugh has done me good,” said Nott, after a pause ; “ but do you think there is no chance of Miss Rivers refusing to take the black veil ? ”

“ I should be sorry to buoy you up with false hopes, Captain Nott,” replied Ella. “ It was her earnest desire to enter the convent ; and although she might legally retract her vows at the end of her year of probation, and come again to us, yet it is well known such cases are extremely rare. It is the endeavour of all in a convent to retain those who have once been resident there ; and I fear every impediment would be thrown in the way of her reclaiming her liberty. Besides, to a disposition like poor Grace’s, the quiet, monotonous routine would not be distasteful, and, as a novice, she would be very kindly

* A positive fact.

used, and, even if she broke rules, treated with great lenity. I much fear that Grace would be loth to sever herself from a life she has so long looked forward to."

"The devil of it is," said Seymour, heedless of Ella's admonishing "hush," "that the abbess is so absolute. Everything is as she wills, and none in the convent dare interfere with her authority. How such places are permitted to exist in England, without being liable to some Government inspection, I cannot imagine. It has been found necessary to look after all other communities, and persons having charge of others. All sorts of dreadful atrocities have, for instance, been committed on lunatics, even in these times, and the press has brought more than one to light."

How unjust, how wicked it is, to impose an oath upon a very young girl, binding her for life to a convent's walls, making her shirk the true duties, the true aspirations of life.

CHAPTER XV.

SUSPENSE.

" And shall we all condemn and all distrust
Because some men are false and some unjust?
Forbid it Heaven; for better 'twere to be
Duped of the fond impossibility—
Of light and radiance which sleep's visions gave,
Than thus to live suspicions bitter slave."

HON. MRS. NORTON.

SORROWFUL as Percy and Ella were at what their relative had done, Captain Nott's silent grief was far more bitter. He had hoped against hope; he had witnessed in that dark silent agony that tears refuse to assuage, the ceremony we have detailed in our previous chapter, and had listened with saddened heart to the words of the venerable archbishop, " Receive the white veil the emblem of purity, that thou mayest follow the Lamb without spot, and mayest

walk with him in white, in the name of the
Father, and of the Son, and of the Holy
Ghost." His feelings were, perhaps, stung
to a higher intensity than would, have been
the case with many a young man, because
Captain Nott—to use a worldly phrase—was
a strong Protestant. He realized, and truly
felt the force of our Redeemer's act, in not
taking his chosen followers out of the world,
but praying that they might be preserved
pure and spotless in the midst of a sinful
generation, amongst whom they were to be
bright and shining beacons of the hope that
lay in them. Captain Nott, moreover, had
read much about, and pondered deeply
upon, monastic and convent systems—and
had arrived at the conclusion, that however
desirable they might have been in the middle
ages, as places of refuge from the lawless
knights and their followers, who swarmed in
those times, the people who *now* retired from
the world into the cloister, shirked the true
duties, temptations, and trials it is part of
God's all wise provision that mankind are to
experience. He considered also, that, how-

ever agreeable it is to the senses to be continually engaged in the absorbing service of the mass, to be listening to, or taking part in anthems, in the sweet music that morning, noon, and night re-echoes through convent walls—it was for a higher and holier purpose that God has placed men and women here. True it is, he considered, that some people are holy, others are wicked ; but the former are ever found to cultivate the hidden inner life of purity that dwells within them, and far from shunning the business and the toils of every day, they cheerfully performed their daily labour, though not bound by any artificial vow.

Captain Nott, in spite of his misery and his unhappiness endeavoured not to look upon life as a blank, but roused himself to attend to his duties in the position he had earned by a long course of diligent study. About this time, too, his attention was diverted from Grace Rivers, by an order to change his station and duties. Though sorry to quit Hampshire, and the neighbourhood of Strange Hall, he left it in a frame of mind that many, under the circumstances, would have envied. He felt certain that what had happened was for some wise purpose, and would in the end be over-ruled for his good. He also felt cheered by a little poem that Ella had just sent him——a copy of one she had composed for a little cousin——thinking that it could do Captain Nott no harm, and might lead his thoughts into happier channels. We think our readers have as much right to the benefit of our fair heroine's composition as Captain Nott, so here is her poetry——written during a country walk :——

I.

" I saw in my walk a beautiful lark,
  Rise up from the grassy sod,
 It pour'd forth its tuneful lay as it rose,
  And seemed to sing praises to God.

II.

" Methought that it chanted a hymn of delight,
  To the Maker of all that's fair,
 Risen up from earth, its conflicts and cares,
  Warbling hymns amidst waves of air.

III.

" At length it became but a speck in the sky,
  Soon fading away from sight,
 Its notes faintly fell on my listening ear,
  Borne on zephyr breeze so light.

IV.

" Sweet bird, merry songster, thou teachest to me,
  Lessons of love and delight,
May I soar like thee from the realms of earth,
  To the land veiled from mortal sight.

V.

" May I soar above earth, its toils, its cares,
  Its conflicts of strife and pain,
Rise to the knowledge of Christ and his love,
  And more of Him daily attain."

---

* From original unpublished MSS.

CHAPTER XVI.

CAPTAIN NOTT TAKES A HOLIDAY.

" Alone, alone, let me wander alone ;
There's an odour of hay o'er the woodlands blown ;
There's a humming of bees beneath the lime,
And the deep blue heaven of a southern clime
Is not more beautifully bright
Than this English sky with its islets white,
And its Alp-like clouds, so snowy fair—
The birch leaves dangle in balmy air ;
And the elms and oaks scarce seem to know
When the whispering breezes come and go."
                                        DR. MACKAY.

IN a few days Captain Nott was at his
new station, and entered upon his new
employment of building an observatory.
From a combination of trifles, he and his
new chief unfortunately did not work in that
harmonious manner which is ever conducive
to the interests of business ; and our hero,
finding all his efforts to do right were
continually opposed, contented himself by

giving—as he termed it—a piece of his mind to his tormentor, and doing his utmost to live peaceably with him, and with all men. Time passed along, and by slow degrees disease laid its grasp upon Captain Nott. He struggled against it, but it would not go, and at length it became apparent to his friends, and at last to himself, that he was becoming seriously ill. He endeavoured to procure a respite from his labours, but without success ; and not unnaturally thought that former animosities, added to a resistance he had made to become a resident in a low village pot-house, weighed against his obtaining the desired boon. At last he consulted his medical adviser, from whom he received every attention and every kindness that it was possible to afford.

Captain Nott's illness, though serious, did not much affect his personal appearance ; and his doctor told him very candidly that although every day he remained at his work he was becoming worse, still there was a certain amount of etiquette to be observed, be the consequences what they might, and that

he must remain under medical treatment for
a certain time, and then go on sick leave.
This, of course, Captain Nott did ; in fact he
had fallen into a morose state of mind, and
really cared very little about what took place,
and at length went off to Southampton. The
day after his arrival he went to consult a doctor,
who, amongst other remedies, recommended
him to go out on the beach, and enjoy the
fresh sea breeze. He sauntered up and down,
but could not at first avoid taking a jaundiced
view of affairs in general, and strolled to
the pier to await the arrival of the mail train
from London. He sat there awhile, watching
the merry groups of children at play, the
nurse maids coquetting with the soldiers, the
bathing machines high above the water, and
the flotilla of schooners, brigs, skiffs, and
boats in the offing. The powerful steamer
now drew in to the pier, for the London
express was momentarily expected ; at length
down rushed the train, and a stream of passengers poured forth. But who was that
group of nuns, and who was that lovely fair
young girl, whose features, careworn either

from mental or bodily anguish, were so painful to behold ?   No madness, no weak intellect, was apparent in her countenance.
She was hurried down the steps of the pier,
and it was apparent that her limbs were
firmly secured, while one of her jailors had
flung an arm tightly round her throat to
prevent her cries for help. Captain Nott
with great difficulty forced his way to her ;
it was *not* Sister Grace. He implored the
bystanders to advance to her rescue, but his
entreaties were unavailing, and he alone was
unable to prevent her being forced on board
the steamer. When she arrived upon the
deck, the grasp upon her neck was relaxed,
and her thrilling shrieks might well have
melted the hearts of the most obdurate. A
few seconds afterwards she was forced below,
and Captain Nott turned from the spot with
an aching heart, bitterly lamenting his old
company had not been on the pier.

His fears for the safety of Sister Grace
were now redoubled ; for he felt sure that the
poor victim of to-day had been hurried away
from England, lest inquiry might bring to

light some deed of darkness that might have brought condign punishment upon the perpetrators.

Captain Nott, however, had the satisfaction of observing, a few days afterwards, that the *Daily Mercury* had noticed the outrage, and through its columns demanded that the occurrence should be sifted. Seymour, too, made his appearance at Southampton ; he had come there chiefly to see what his brother officer was doing. The conversation naturally turned upon the painful sight Captain Nott had seen, and Seymour remarked, " It may be all very well to have Roman Catholic institutions in England ; but when we have reason to suspect that violence and fraud are practised upon their inmates, and the directors of those establishments are accused of wickedness and abduction in a public journal, it is only to be expected that those interested, should rebut the accusation. If they fail to do so, or maintain silence, they must not be astonished if public opinion demands a searching investigation."

" Exactly so," replied Nott. " Protestants

are generally disposed to tolerate *all* religious bodies, and if Roman Catholics fan the embers of religious discord they are very silly, and they may depend they certainly will not escape with impunity if they infringe in England 'the liberty of the subject.' "

Captain Seymour returned to Strange Hall that day, leaving his brother officer to his own thoughts.

Disgusted with most things, Captain Nott now bent his steps to London, and went to the Crystal Palace. He wandered in dreamy pleasure through the dazzling courts ; watched the great fountains play ; listened to the pealing organ that poured soft melody along the glittering building ; and then sat down in the lofty dining hall, and ate his luncheon. Then he felt better, and in a more genial temper, and could appreciate the system and order that prevailed in the room, and watched for awhile some old fellow in a funny little square box, busily engaged in some mysterious process—probably making out the little bills for the company. Then Captain Nott walked about the grounds admiring the parterres of flowers ; the verdure of the cricket ground ; the sparkling lake, where reposed restored monsters of a long past age ; went and shot for some nuts, and had a ride in one of the merry-go-rounds. Finding he had a spare half-hour he took a trip on the Pneumatic passenger railway, and inspected, with a professional eye, the working of the machinery in all its details. He saw how a vast disc creates such a blast, that a heavy carriage, crowded with passengers, is blown through a tunnel after the same fashion that he used to blow peas through his pea-shooter when at school, and how on the return journey the carriage was, as it were, sucked through the tube, and he was again at the place he had started from a few minutes before.

He returned to London that evening, his journey being enlivened by the vagaries of a school-mistress, who, with her French governess, was likewise returning in charge of her flock of eighteen school girls. She evidently regarded Captain Nott and a mild inoffensive old gentleman who had presumed to enter the carriage before her as two dangerous characters, and inflicted a severe lecture upon the guard for his improper conduct in not having preserved a whole first-class carriage for herself and tribe. This discourse was ended by that functionary blowing his whistle and the train starting. The good school-mistress then poured into Captain Nott's ear her doubts and fears for the safety of "madame," and the six young ladies under *her* charge, and how excessively wicked the railway company were to have allowed her school to be separated on their journey, and mixed up with unknown gentlemen. Captain Nott with great difficulty preserved his gravity, agreed with the good lady that the conduct of the railway company was indeed naughty, and by this time the train stopped at an intermediate station. The old lady's head was immediately thrust out of the window, and a long conversation held with "madame" in the next carriage, greatly to the delight of the railway porters, our hero, and the young ladies in *his* carriage ; the conversation of course terminated by the train starting ; and the school-mistress became almost frantic because " madame " had told her there was *one* vacant place in *her* carriage, and persisted in declaring that it would soon be occupied by some dreadful man.   Captain Nott then behaved very badly, and horrified the school-mistress, and perhaps the young ladies, by asking if any one knew what horse was likely to win next year's Derby.

After he had remained a few days in London he went to spend the rest of his leave at Strange Hall.

CHAPTER XVII.

SISTER GRACE TAKES THE BLACK VEIL.

" For aye to be in shady cloister mew'd.
'To live a barren sister all your life,
Chanting faint hymns to the cold fruitless moon."
SHAKESPEARE.

MORE than a year glided quietly away ; and for
the last time we present that church, already
so familiar to our readers, in the exhibition of
one of the most solemn of ceremonials——the
profession, or taking the black veil.

It was nearly the end of the double-faced
month of February. The trees in the dark
woods were stretching their lank arms, as if,
in supplication to the sky, they were bewailing
their leaves. The day was showery, but calm,
and interspersed with many a gleam of sun-
shine. The rivulets, nay the river flowing
before the Hall, were swollen, and a favourite

N 2

snipe marsh was ancle deep in snow water,
through which coarse grass bobbed and
waved.

Ella and Percy walked through the domain towards the church; the snowdrop
peeped forth in some sheltered situations, and
signs of the approaching season were around
them. The coltsfoot bloomed gaily, and pale
flushes of green tinted the buds that a week
before were brown. Other wee floral treasures
lay around; all appeared tranquil and calm.
The winter aconite was opening its golden
yellow or pale blue blossoms, and the delicate
primrose and early violet reposed in stray
nooks. Merry brown hares and gay rabbits
skipped across their path.

Ella stopped to gather some violets. "The
sweetest of flowers, Percy, are hid here. Stay,
I feel I can compose some lines on this; my
poetical spirit has been long absent. I feel it
returning," and she warbled :——

I.
"How oft we see the sweetest flowers,
Bloom in sequestered dells,
Far, far removed from public gaze,
Like monks within their cells.

II.

"Thus as in nature we oft find,
　　Those who possess Christ's grace
Who his devoted servants are,
　　Upheld in life's long race.

III.

"Frequently placed in humble walks,
　　To fortune and to fame,
Alike unknown they are content,
　　They seek not more to gain.

IV.

"They *feel* the truth, yet they have not
　　Heard the good poet's lay,
The calm retreat, the silent shade,
　　With prayer and praise agree.

V.

"Their life is hid with Christ in God,
　　And when He shall appear,
They'll shine like Him in glory bright,
　　For they have cost Him dear."*

By this time they had reached the church, which was rapidly filling, and in this instance mass was celebrated. Sister Grace communicated at it, and the sisterhood into which she was to be enrolled walked in procession, with lighted candles, round the sacred edifice. The black veil lying near the altar, with the act of profession ready for Sister Grace's signature,

* From original unpublished MSS.

made Ella visibly shudder, and heartily repent she had not withheld her consent. Time for reflection had, however, gone by, and the hymn—

"Come Holy Ghost, Creator come."

was sweetly sung by the choir.

The three priests, who officiated in those remarkable mysteries, were robed in vestments of cloth of gold, and their devotional feelings were evidently deeply impressed with the solemnity of the ceremonial. And now the archbishop's arrival at the chapel-door was announced.

Grace Rivers in her novice's dress, her white veil thrown back, and holding in her hand a lighted taper, as by a miracle appeared kneeling above the high altar. Ella and Seymour, who occupied seats directly in its front, were for the first time made aware there was a grating there, which would, when closed, represent the wall. Grace held in her other hand a black crucifix, upon which she steadily gazed.

Ella burst into an agony of grief, as Grace

for an instant turned towards her with an expression of natural emotion.

Nott, who was present, was also strongly affected at the sight he witnessed ; for as all are aware, Grace had long been the cherished idol of his affections, and he had clung to the hope she would not take this final step. Grace caught Nott's agonised expression, and gently bent her head in token of recognition.

The kneeling girl was thrown into strong relief by the white roof of the richly embellished inner chapel, which with its tapestry and beautiful hangings extended far behind her.

Every eye was rivetted upon her, as she knelt for the irrevocable step. The archbishop passed to the altar, before which he knelt some minutes in prayer, and sprinkled the veil with holy water, saying, *In nomine Patris, et Filii et Spiritus Sancti ;* then taking his seat, his attendants disrobed him of his scarlet robe, and attired him in his episcopal vestments of silver tissue, trimmed with fringe and edgings of gold.

He at length was seen vested in cope and

mitre, and holding his shepherd's crook.——
He sprinkled the ring with holy water.
Father Francis, who had returned, and was,
pro tem., the confessor to the convent, kissed
his hand, and publicly addressed Grace
upon the step she was about to take. His
manner was kindly and warm-hearted; but the
blasphemy which tainted his oration was distressing to his Protestant hearers. He told
Grace, " that the livery she was about to
assume was that of Jesus Christ ; that to him
she would this day be wedded ; that having
rejected the love of an earthly husband "——
(with marked emphasis in his tone for which
Nott mentally vowed vengeance)——" she there-
by preserved her virgin state ; would become
as an angel in heaven, and at her death St.
Peter would at once open to her the gates of
Paradise."

His address ended, the archbishop engaged
in prayer, and Grace vanished from the grate.
She came before the altar, and knelt in front
of the archbishop.

" My child," said he, " what do you demand ? "

" My lord," answered she, " I most humbly beg to be received to the holy profession."

" My child," he inquired, " do you consider yourself sufficiently instructed in what regards the vows of religion, and the rules and constitutions of this institute ; and do you know the obligations you contract by the holy profession ? "

" Yes, my lord, with the grace of God."

" May God," he answered, " grant you perseverance in this your holy resolution, and may he deign in his mercy to consummate what he has begun, in the name of the Father, and of the Son, and of the Holy Ghost."

Turning towards the altar, the archbishop laying aside the cope and mitre, was vested for the celebration of mass. On this occasion the mass of the Holy Ghost was said, and special prayers were offered up in it for Sister Grace.

At length a hymn was chanted; and as the sacred sounds died away, the archbishop again knelt in prayer. After the lapse of some minutes, from the vast depths of the nunnery, the voices of those invisible ones

over whom the veil of mystery is drawn,
rose deliciously softened by distance, in
ineffable sweetness, gradually swelling in
intensity as they approached.

Once more was the panel withdrawn, and
Grace was before the hushed assemblage. She
was kneeling as motionless as a statue; her
white veil raised, and drooping over her
shoulders. Beside her stood two nuns wear-
ing the black veil.

The bishop, who was present, rose and asked
her some questions; but in so low a tone that
neither the questions nor replies were audible.
She retired, and almost immediately a side-
door opened, and she stood in the aperture.

The archbishop went to her, touched her,
sprinkling her with holy water, and in a firm
but scarcely audible voice, the irrevocable
words were pronounced by the deluded girl,
the sacrament being held up before her eyes.

" In the name of our Lord and Saviour
Jesûs Christ, and under the protection of His
immaculate mother, Mary, ever virgin, I, Grace
Rivers, called in religion Sister Grace, do vow
and promise to God, poverty, chastity, and

obedience, and the service of the poor, sick, and ignorant, and to persevere until death in this institute, according to its approved rule and constitutions, under the authority, and in presence of you, my lord, and most reverend father in God, and of our reverend mother superior of this convent, this 26th day of February, 18——." She concluded by signing the act of profession, and received the Holy Communion, accompanied by these words :—— " What God hath commenced in thee, may He himself perfect ; and may the body of our Lord Jesus Christ preserve thy soul unto everlasting life. Amen."

Nott did not attempt to conceal his emotion, and sobbed like a child as Sister Grace appeared on her knees at the grating above the altar ; no more a novice in the white veil, but a professed nun in the black. She had taken that final step the longest life could not retrace. She was now a recluse, an anchorite until death ; for the words :—— " Receive the holy veil, the emblem of chastity and modesty, which mayest thou carry before the judgment seat of our Lord Jesus Christ, that thou mayest have eternal life, and mayest live for ever and ever. Amen."——had been spoken. She calmly uttered one or two stereotyped sentences, and then the music pealed, the choir chanting :——" Come, my beloved, come to be espoused ; the winter is passed, the voice of the turtle is heard, and the flowering vines yield their sweet perfume."

Once more the devoted girl knelt before the archbishop, who taking the ring from the altar, placed it on the third finger of her left hand, saying, " I espouse thee to Jesus Christ, the Son of the Father most high, who shall preserve thee inviolate. Receive, therefore, this ring, the seal of faith and of the Holy Ghost, that thou mayest be called the spouse of God. And if thou shalt serve Him faith-fully thou shalt be crowned for ever."

Rising from her knees, Sister Grace replied in faint accents, " I am espoused to Him whom the angels serve, whose beauty the sun and moon admire." As she retired, she sang alternately with the choir the sentences usual on these occasions, commencing, " My heart hath uttered a good thing; I speak my words to the King."

Finally, she was relieved of the taper she carried, and lying prostrate, the archbishop knelt before the altar, while the *Te Deum* was sung to some of Mozart's soul inspiring music.

The two nuns alluded to suddenly advanced, and stood on either side of Grace, who was still bent in prayer. They lifted the black veil from her face, and arranged it that it fell gracefully over her shoulders. They then placed a gorgeous golden crown of airy and graceful elegance upon her head. Grace still knelt. The spectacle was branded for life on those who beheld it. She held her crucifix in one hand, her taper in the other; her face was plainly seen beneath the golden crown which adorned her. Alas! she was hopelessly immured.

Once more did the archbishop sprinkle her with holy water—then pronounced upon the congregation the benediction. Grace withdrew from the grating, which now resumed its every day aspect.

Ella implored the archbishop to let her embrace Grace once more, and he did not like to refuse the unusual request, for Ella was beloved by the Roman Catholics in the neighbourhood for her charity and goodness.

"What good can it do you to see her, Mrs. Seymour?" said he, in a tone of remonstrance.

"Ah, we were once such friends! I must kiss her again; and I want to give her this keepsake," said she, drawing from her pocket the "Glories of Mary."

The archbishop scrutinised the book. "I wish you believed in these things," he said at length.

"I am thankful that I have seen their darkness," replied she; "but as poor Grace believes in them, let me give her this."

His lordship withdrew, returning shortly with Grace and the abbess. "My daughter," said he, "Mrs. Seymour has somewhat to bestow upon you. I grant you my license to accept it."

The abbess and the archbishop left them together, and walked down the now deserted chapel.

" Oh, my darling, why have you done this ?" sobbed Ella; " Promise me, promise me if they injure you you will send me word; or escape and come to me."

" How can I ?" said Grace, tearfully.

" You know the place better than I do; but I dare say some of the attendants are not beyond a bribe. Here is money," said Ella, giving her twenty sovereigns; "and here, too, is a book, which I do not want you to read; but here is another," said she, giving her the New Testament, " which is worth far more than all missals and manuals. Read it, darling, and believe what it says. The abbess only knows I am giving you the ' Glories of Mary,' but you heard the archbishop give you leave to accept what I gave you. Hide this," said she, pointing to the Testament.

Grace mechanically obeyed her, and embracing her in silence, Ella signed to the abbess, who approached.

" Be kind to her, lady," said she. " Here are ten pounds for the poor of your convent."

CHAPTER XVIII.

FIRE AT STRANGE CONVENT.

"All desp'rate hazards courage do create;
As he plays frankly who has least estate;
Presence of mind, and courage in distress,
Are more than armies to procure success."

DRYDEN.

Now a permanent occupant of the convent, Sister Grace entered with spirit into the unvarying routine. Part of her duty, and to her a very agreeable one, was to teach the pupils drawing. Some months thus glided by; but gradually a yearning desire grew upon her to see her relations at Strange, once more take part in their happy useful life, and assist Seymour and Ella in doing good amongst the tenantry.

Ella's baby (which had after her been named Grace) had been born shortly after she had taken the black veil, and Sister Grace would gladly have aided its youthful mother in its care. Imperceptibly also the plain truths of the gospel, which her friends had so prayerfully instilled, strengthened their grasp upon her mind, and, though perplexed by doubts and fears, the idea continually fluttered across her that she had been placed in this world for a better purpose than to spend her days as she was then doing, in a circle of prayers to the Virgin Mary and numerous other saints. She attempted to curb her rebellious thoughts by dwelling upon the solemnity of her dedication to a cloister life, but it would not bring her peace; and a year after she had become a nun she bitterly mourned in secret that she had pursued the bent of her inclinations, and listened to the insinuating language of Father Francis with a more willing ear than to Seymour's friendly representations, and Ella's sorrowful expostulations. To all outward appearance none in the convent were more devout than she, and her duties were performed with an alacrity and ability second to none. Prayer with sister Grace had never been a mere lip service; it was to her a pleasure, not a duty.

She wondered Ella never came to see her, but she little knew that her cousin had more than once endeavoured to obtain an interview, and illness had been pleaded by way of excuse.

She inquired after Seymour and Ella when she saw Father Francis one day after confession, but could only ascertain they were well and happy. She begged him to invite Ella to come and see her; he promised to do so, but her cousin came not, and Sister Grace soon felt confident that her message had not been delivered. Too fearful to breathe her suspicions to any, and sadly convinced of their truth, she asked permission to visit Ella at Strange Hall. She was sternly refused, and closely questioned as to her motives; but whatever Father Francis or the abbess conjectured, they elicited nothing beyond the bare fact that she was very anxious to see Ella.

From that day, however, Sister Grace felt she was under surveillance, and regarded with suspicion. It is, perhaps, needless to dilate in detail upon the combination of oppression

and unkindness which determined Sister Grace
to free herself at all hazards from the thral-
dom in which she was detained. She had,
however, apparently no prospect of success.
No authorised authority, save that appointed
by the high dignitaries of the Romish Church,
visited the convent; none were empowered to
inquire into the doings within its walls; to
listen to, or redress any well grounded com-
plaint of an inmate. Sister Grace felt that to
her, indeed, applied with agonising power, the
words, "All ye who enter here abandon hope."
The summer was speedily waning, when one
evening the inmates of the convent were
thrown into consternation by an alarm of fire.
Volumes of smoke encompassed the building;
but it was soon discovered that "wolf" had
been called too loudly, and only the chimney
of the refectory was burning. Various were
the suggestions for extinguishing the flames,
until Father Francis' sudden presence enforced
silence. That ubiquitous person produced a
large horn of powder, and fired a small charge
in the chimney; and the flames subsided.
While attention was confined to his doings,

Sister Grace, who with the other nuns were silently looking on, emptied a quantity of the gunpowder into a tumbler, which stood upon the table, concealed it in her dress, retired noiselessly, and secreted it in her cell. She had some days before with a little trouble, aided by a hammer, pincers, and three or four knives, raised a board in the floor, and in the hiding place there obtained, deposited her treasure. She then patiently waited her time.

CHAPTER XIX.

A PIC-NIC TO PLACE HOUSE.

"Titchfield stream is calm—a crowd of sunny faces,
And plumed heads, and shoulders round and white,
Are mirror'd in the waters.   There are traces
Of merriment in those sweet eyes of light—
Lie empty hampers round ; in shady places
The hungry throw themselves with ruthless might
On lobster salads ; while champagne to cheer 'em,
Cools in the brook that murmurs sweetly near 'em."

Altered from COLLINS.

ELLA's thoughts frequently reverted to her cousin, but she had no idea of her state of mind.   A large party of visitors were staying at the Hall, and she resolved to take her guests on a pic-nic excursion to Place House, a fine old ruin in Hampshire, which had once belonged to the Earls of Southampton, but now a portion of the estate of H. Delme, Esq. The ill-fated King Charles I. had slept there on his journey to Carisbrook Castle, and in these days it is a favourite "meet" for the Humbleton hounds, and the resort of pic-nic and sketching parties, who love the old broken-down ruin.

To Place House, accordingly, they went. The drive was a long but not a weary one, for Hampshire, in May, well deserves what the author of "Autumn Leaves," with a little variation, has said of the month :—

> "May, May, song-honoured May,
> Whom the youthful poet has loved alway,
> Lovely, indeed, is thy genial air,
> Thy voices of music everywhere,
> The blessed blue of thy kindly skies,
> Thy bloom that greets us with sweet surprise,
> The hedgerow covered with odorous snow,
> Thy waters that laugh with joy as they go."

What kind of a day greeted the excursionists ? Well, it was a day after rain, but the soft wind had mellowed the temperature, and the sun gleamed through the patches of clouds. The hedges on their course had brought out their spring array of green ; over it the white thorn had curled in dense clusters of snowy blossoms. Along the hedgerows and banks, bouquets of flowers swayed to each passing zephyr, or nestled in the abundant grass, fragrant with the buttercup and crowsfoot, diffused through it in glittering patches. But Place House was reached; the equipage lodged at the nearest hostelrie, and the various good things stowed in hampers were brought to view. One section of the party undertook to lay dinner, under the far-famed oak tree of the grounds, which, even in decaying age, threw forth its foliage. Others were anxious to minutely inspect the ruin; and one party of sketchers, headed by a gentleman who dearly prized the beautiful in art and nature, transferred the old turrets to paper; he, however, making an exquisite sketch in oils of the old tree. Nor were admirers wanting for the meadows bright with their vernal mantle, and redolent of delicate flowers, permeated by the river chill and calm; in its bubbling waters one of the party angled awhile for trout; they rose so freely that he soon killed half a dozen. Ella had quitted those who were spreading the luncheon, and went in search of some truants, whom she believed to be lingering about the old house. She hastened, by mistake, into a court-yard overgrown with nettles, and as she was turning back she felt herself grasped by a figure in black, closely veiled. Her first impulse was to shriek for help ; but the figure, perhaps seeing her terror, released her, and said hastily : " Sister Grace is in danger from what she did last night to escape. Be discreet." The figure was withdrawing, when Ella, with an almost supernatural effort, gasped, " Where is she now ? " " I know not ; she is in danger," was the reply. Some of the party now approaching, the figure brushed hastily by, and seemed as if by magic to vanish.

The young ladies rallied Ella upon the strange companion with whom she had been conversing ; but, escaping from them, she sought her husband. Seymour laughed at her fears ; but in reality he was considerably alarmed, and bidding her apologise to the guests, said he " would hunt up all about the matter ;" and mounting a spare horse, rode hastily to the house of the chief of the police of the district. Whatever passed we can only at present conjecture ; but that evening, and for some time afterwards, the railway station and the approaches to the neighbourhood of the convent were narrowly guarded by those courteous men in " blue." Ella, feeling that all was in safe hands, did the honours of the open air banquet to perfection. The brilliancy of the day seemed to increase as the hours glided on. Some of the party took a hasty walk to Heathfield, and meeting its hospitable owner, accompanied as usual by his two four-footed aides-de-camp, " Ginger" and " Spice," accepted his invitation to ramble over his lovely grounds and garden. From them they viewed the chalk mounds which glistened in the distance on Portsdown Hill, marking the site of the *cordon* of forts which will shortly bid defiance to the strong man ; for one stronger than he is armed, and will, with divine help, keep his goods and his dockyard in peace.

The waning sun at length warned all the tourists to return ; and orders had been sent for the carriages, when a woman passed with a something in her arms, but whether a doll

or baby, the party were divided in their opinion.
She, however, placed it beyond doubt by toss-
ing the doll (which it really was) in the air,
after a fashion that no baby could have endured, and laughed heartily at the amazement
of the majority, who had declared in favour of
the "baby." Then some of the ladies secreted wine bottles in a crevice of the time-
worn building, conjecturing that they might
some day perchance to fall into the hands of
savant explorers; and then the merry party
returned to Strange Hall. When they arrived
they heard the nightingale in full "throated
ease," in the shrubberies.

I.
" And deep was the silence, unbroken and still,
　　As they listened in breathless delight,
　The moonbeams lay soft on the side of the hill,
　　Melting into the shadows of night.

II.
" And hushed was the valley, and hushed was Strange lake,
　　No leaf in the forest now stirred,
　No sound but the moan of the ripples that break,
　　On the glistening pebbles was heard.

III.
" At length a low cadence, and now a clear trill,
　　And now a full gush of rich song,
　Burst forth in the distance, and then all was still,
　　Save the echo which floated along."

The reapers of, perhaps, the only May crop—willow beds—returning with bundles of osiers, at length startled the songsters, and they ceased their lays.

Ella's state of mind was most unenviable, though, for the sake of others, she endeavoured to appear cheerful. With all her efforts she continually found herself brooding upon her old presentiment,—that something dreadful would arise out of the pic-nic to Place House. How far she was correct we shall now soon learn.

CHAPTER XX.

THE ESCAPE.

> " All the elements
> At least had gone to wreck, disturbed and torn
> With violence of this conflict, had not soon
> Th'Eternal hung His golden scales."
>
> MILTON.

A FEW evenings afterwards Sister Grace had completed her preparations, and unseen by any of her sisters, slipped away as they were returning from midnight mass. She had frequently heard Seymour and Nott converse about what she was about to attempt, and had seen one or two experiments at Strange, to test their theories. She had prepared two long paper tubes, which she filled with gunpowder, and secured them in the folds of her dress. The night was dark, but she knew every inch of the ground she was treading, and glided fleetly across the burial acre. She reached, without molestation, a strong wooden door, which had been inserted in the high wall for Father Francis' convenience; once beyond this, she was free. She cautiously felt for the key-hole, and shook the contents of one of her paper tubes into it; then pushing the other in as far as possible, she covered the end with gunpowder, slightly moistened, and struck a light against the brick wall. A gust of wind instantly extinguished it; but using her dress as a shield she contrived to light the damp powder, and stepped behind a convenient yew-tree. The train fizzed and spluttered until it reached the dry powder,—then a lurid glare, a sharp sound, and then all was still. In an agony of suspense Sister Grace rushed to the door. The wood work round the lock was shattered. She was free! She soon made her way into the high road, and walked hurriedly in the direction of Strange Hall. In a short time, however, the glancing of torches to and fro, and the noise behind her, made the unhappy girl aware her pursuers were at hand. In her flight she passed by a cottage, and caught sight of the

open door, into which a gentleman was entering.   She   rushed   to   him ;   it   was   Captain
Nott.   The truth at once flashed across him.
He dragged the fainting girl into his sitting-
room. He and his servant speedily barred the
door and windows, and from a back window,
the faithful Hamilton (for he it was) rushed
to the temporary telegraph that had been
erected to enable his master to communicate
expeditiously with his detachment, and ap-
prised them of the danger.   The door, meanwhile, was saluted with kicks, and demands
for admission ; but Nott, taking no notice
of the demand, locked all the doors of the
rooms on the ground floor, hastily barricaded
the stairs with a few articles of furniture ; and
taking Sister Grace into an upper room,
loaded his fowling piece, and proceeded to
parley with the invaders from a window, his
great object being to gain time.   They demanded instant admission, declaring they
knew the young lady to be there ; and Nott,
after trying cajoleries and every means he
could devise to check their inroad and gain
time, at length—as they were proceeding to

burst in the door with a sledge-hammer, which had just then been brought—warned them that he had loaded fire arms, and would use them if they entered. No heed, however, was paid to his threats; the door at length gave way, and in rushed the retainers of the convent. Nott, however, kept his word. He aimed low; the two foremost fell under his fire. He attempted to reload, but a rush made on the stairs swept away the roughly formed barrier, and he had barely time to retreat into the apartment where Sister Grace was ensconced, ere his pursuers were on the upper floor. While they were knocking down the slight wooden door, he had reloaded his gun, and when the door was dashed in he was prepared for a second double shot. The assailants paused; none liked to be the man to receive the fire, and the party, now reduced to twelve, drew slightly back. At this instant, however, the bugle of the approaching detachment pierced shrilly through the night air, and the sight of Sister Grace, standing behind Nott, re-animated the convent retainers. An onward rush was

made—two more fell.   Nott flung the silver
candlestick at a third, shouted loudly for help,
broke his gun on a fourth, and dashed, armed
with a chair, upon a fifth.   His desperate
resistance availed him not ; a heavy blow on
the head sent him to the ground, and if the
footsteps of his detachment had not that
instant been heard outside, it would have
fared very ill with him.

Nott's sergeant and a party of men entered
the house, as Sister Grace, with a gag over
her mouth, was being forced down the stairs.
The leader explained that Captain Nott " had
inveigled his daughter," (as he had the imper-
tinence to call Sister Grace) " into his quarters,
and that he was only taking her home."

This explanation was not satisfactory to
the sergeant, and he was about to direct his
men to detain the interlopers, when Hamilton
called loudly for help for his master, and in
the confusion, aided by the darkness, the
invading band escaped, carrying Sister Grace,
and all the wounded men away with them.

Two of the detachment were despatched to
procure the nearest medical aid for Captain

Nott, whose head was severely cut and bruised. Next morning he was better, and sent to Strange Hall for Seymour; but before the message arrived there, our hero, as we are aware, had gone to Place House, and from the mysterious stranger came the first intimation of what had occurred. In the evening, however, Seymour came to see Nott; their conversation was prolonged far into night, and Nott's friend quitted him in a very angry of mind, vowing vengeance on the convent, and all connected with it.

Seymour had too great a horror of the delay of the law to resort to its aid for rescuing Sister Grace from the clutches of the convent authorities, if, indeed, the law would have interfered at all; but his local influence and his purse effected what he wanted, —that the convent should be vigilantly guarded to prevent her secret removal. The threat which had been held over Ella, of stealthily conveying her to an Italian convent, had suggested to Seymour that this might be attempted with Sister Grace. He longed, indeed, that the attempt should be made, as he had quite determined to assail her protectors, and convey her to Strange Hall. No such good fortune, however, favoured his longings, and he was at his wits' end when a letter was brought about day break to the hall. The butler, roused by the knocking, got up and opened the door on the chain. The letter was pushed in, and the messenger instantly made her escape, deaf to the vociferations of the portly menial "to stop." Whatever were the contents of the missive, certain is it that Seymour left the Hall without his breakfast, to Ella's horror and alarm, when she came down stairs and realized what he had done.

CHAPTER XXI.

THE TRIAL.

" Let rules be fixed that may our rage contain,
And punish faults with a proportioned pain ;
And do not flay him who deserves alone
A whipping for the fault that he has done."

HORACE.

SISTER GRACE and her captors reached the
convent, the former almost dead with exhaus-
tion and fright. The abbess would have at
once confined her in the vault of penitence,
but Father Francis interfered, and she was
placed in her own cell. The next morning
she was very ill, and had to be removed to the
infirmary. She was not long permitted to
enjoy its comparative quiet, but was brought
back to the convent, and, as a preliminary
measure, was removed at midnight from her
cell and confined in the vault of penitence for
twenty-four hours. A piece of bread, but

P 2

no water, was allowed her. She bore this better than the abbess expected, and the following midnight she was released, blindfolded, and partly led, partly carried, she knew not whither, and her hands were tied behind her. When the bandage was removed she was in a low gloomy cavern, the roof apparently supported by irregular arches, damp with time. A few gravestones, with obliterated inscriptions, were scattered over the floor. She realised that she was in the place she had only heard of in the most vague tradition——she had doubted its existence——the burial-ground for such as had died in mortal sin. An iron table stood in the centre of this dismal territory; upon it lay a ponderous volume. She knew it, for she had seen it in the abbess's apartment. It was the rules of the order of which she had sworn to be a nun. She became as white as ashes, and almost sank in the ground as she recognised this volume; for she realised she was about to be tried for her life. Round the iron table sat a solemn conclave——Father Francis, the abbess, and some one she had never seen; but from his age,

appearance, and dress, she judged he must be
a high dignitary of the Church of Rome.

> " Well might her pallor terror speak,
>   For there was seen in that dark wall,
>   A niche both narrow deep and tall,
>   None entering at that grisly door,
>   Were known to e'er find exit more.
>   In it a slender meal was laid,
>   Of pulse of water and of bread,
>   By it in dark and cowled dress,
>   Three haggard men stood motionless;
>   Each holding high a flaming torch,
>   Lighted th' grim entrance of the porch,
>   Reflecting back the time worn beam,
>   The mouldy walls and arches gleam,
>   Bricks and cement were there display'd,
>   With building tools in order laid."

The sound of cautious footsteps broke the
stillness: six of the nuns were led blindfolded
upon the scene, and when fairly in the mysterious apartment were permitted to witness
what was passing. Sister Grace recognised
them all. They had been brought there to
learn how the Church of Rome dealt with
those who, reckoned amongst the dead,
broke their vows. All was hushed; but at
irregular intervals a dull clang, as of some
distant labour, reached Sister Grace, whose

naturally acute sense of hearing was strung
to a painful intensity.   The abbess broke the
stillness.   " I suppose you will not deny that
you, a professed sister of our order, left the
retreat in which your superior had consigned
you, after your vows, taken freely before the
altar, and were discovered shortly after midnight in the quarters of an unmarried officer? "

" It would be useless if I did; but I would
crave permission to say a few words," said
Sister Grace, with a great effort.

" We will hear you hereafter," said the
unknown Church dignitary.   " Do you admit
the truth of the accusation ? "

" Yes," replied she, in a low tone.   " I fled
into the house where I was found when I heard
my pursuers behind me on the road."   A
pitying shudder ran through the group of witnesses as she spoke.   " It will be unnecessary
to delay further," observed the speaker, and
the conclave held a consultation in such a subdued tone that none heard what passed.

" Unhappy girl, it is now permitted you to
speak," said Father Francis, turning towards
her.

Twice Sister Grace essayed to do so, and twice the words died on her lips. The unknown dignitary rose ; he supposed she had nothing to say in her defence, and was about to pronounce the chapter's sentence. Sister Grace's tongue was suddenly loosened ; in slow measured accents, which gained strength and animation as she proceeded, she addressed them :——

"I presume, as you have brought me here, you have made up your mind what to do with me. I fear not death, in whatever form it may come ; though, had it been permitted me to choose, I would not have selected a long lingering one. As a girl, the doctrines of the Church of Rome were planted in my mind, with all the seductive power that worked, alas, too convincingly on my intellect. I was led to believe the world one vast hospital of sin and misery, and that the only safeguard for bliss hereafter was to shun and totally withdraw from all domestic happiness and active usefulness. Into this retreat I came. Alas ! when I had taken the black veil, the snare into which I had fallen became more

and more apparent as time swept on.   I was
treated in a far different manner than when I
wore the white coif.   I see now clearly the
stubble and hay that the Church of Rome has
heaped upon the true foundation which God
has given to his Church throughout the uni-
verse.   You endeavour to persuade your flock
that they by good works will save themselves.
You do not tell them that the sufferings and
death of our Redeemer, who took into his
divine a human nature, who uttered the cry
of infancy, who was subservient to an earthly
mother, that His hands that first framed all
things, and probably worked at the trade of
his reputed father, has purchased free salvation for all sinners who will freely accept it.
No," continued she, raising her voice, "you do
not.   You are the false teachers who 'forbid to
marry, and to abstain from meats.'   If you, as
the blessed Virgin did, kept in your hearts and
pondered on our Redeemer's sayings, well
would it have been for you.   You can now
work forth your will, I am powerless to hinder
you; yet dread me from my awful tomb, ye
vassal slaves of the Papal See.   I am loved by

many powerful friends in the outer world; think not my fate will be a secret; it will not be long unknown. I can even now," she added wildly, "hear the tramp of my deliverers. I can see the hour approaching when my living tomb will be burst asunder, and bitter, bitter vengeance will be wreaked upon the guilty and the innocent alike, in memory of my cruel fate. The law of England will reach you yet, even if remorse does not. Vainly will you plead the rules of your order before an English court of justice. A dark hour is nearing you. Better that an earthquake should now rend your altar and your chapel than that hour of revenge really arrive. Understand me, I am not sueing for mercy; I know your pitiless natures too well."

The "unknown," who had taken a seat during her address, slowly rose; as he did so a clamour, as of the clanking of chains and armour, was momentarily heard. All present crossed themselves and looked troubled, Sister Grace excepted. "The spirits of the unholy dead are lamenting their torments," said Father Francis solemnly. Again mute silence enthralled the cavern. "Unhappy, guilty sister;" said the unknown, "may thy earthly troubles soon be over. *Vade in pacem.*"

The three figures who had held the torches instantly transferred them to a fourth, who emerged from behind a large fragment of rock. They took hold of Sister Grace; the cord which was tied round her delicate wrists, now discoloured and swollen, was removed, she was roughly pushed into the niche in the wall, and the awful work of walling her up *alive* commenced. Four of the nuns fainted at the spectacle, and the conclave busied themselves in endeavouring to revive them. The work rapidly progressed; a small hole left for air excepted, soon no sign of the niche remained. A long wild shriek of despair rang through the vault, and re-echoed through the gloom. All were mute. A sound of human voices reached the bewildered assembly; as if by magic a fissure appeared in the wall—a crash of stones —a cloud of dust and rubbish completely obscured the cavern, and the guilty judges were surrounded.

"Where is she, child of hell?" yelled Seymour—for he it was—seizing Father Francis by the throat, and shaking him violently.

"I know not," replied he, "what you mean."

"Villain, tell me, or the next minute is your last on earth."

"It is here, sir," exclaimed an intelligent Sapper, who was sounding the walls with a hammer.

"Look to the whole lot of them, they shall never escape the hangman," roared Nott, and the new masonry was speedily cleft in pieces by the wedges and crowbars of the party.

Exclamations of horror burst from the soldiers, as Sister Grace, apparently an inanimate corpse, came in view. Nott and Seymour carefully lifted her up, and laid her on the floor. "She is not *dead*," said the latter, holding in breathless suspense a feather to her lips. "May I live to avenge her!" gasped Nott. "What's the way out of this fiendish den? Tie the whole lot of them, women and all," said he, savagely, turning to the sergeant.

"Heaven knows," said Seymour, "we can

never take her through the place we entered.
What's the way to the upper air, you fiend?"
roared Seymour to Father Francis, who made
no answer.   "You shall tell me or die in
your sins," said Seymour, the most careful
search having failed to discover any means of
exit.   "With ball cartridge load!" cried he,
to a party of six of the men, who instantly
obeyed.   "Put the brute up there," said he,
indicating the spot.   "Ready.   If I say present you will have six ounces of lead through
your wicked hoary head.   Will you tell us
the way out?"   Father Francis articulated,
"yes, if you release me."   "Oh, very well,"
said Seymour, coolly, "release him, and put
a rope round his waist; if he attempts any
treachery, knock him on the head."   Father
Francis went to the table, and signed to
remove it.   When this was done, the ring
bolt of a trap door came in view.   Two of
the Engineers raised this, and discovered a
flight of steps.   "I suppose this is the way
to the upper regions," said Seymour to
Father Francis, who bowed assent.   "Will
you lead the way, and if you play any tricks,

I'll give you a taste of this," slapping the
barrel of his revolver as he spoke. " You
remain here Nott with Grace. Half the men
can stay with you, and I'll take the others
with me."

Without much difficulty, aided by the
dark lanterns the party had brought, they
passed down some winding steps into a
landing. Father Francis opened a door in
the opposite wall, and when he had done
this, Seymour left one of the men to remove
the door from its hinges, for fear of some
unseen treachery. A long flight of stone
steps lay before them, which they ascended;
a door at the top, similar to that at the
bottom, barred further progress; but Father
Francis produced a skeleton key, and pressing a secret spring, they found themselves
in the chapel. The door on the reverse was
a picture of Saint Dominic; and none could
have guessed what was behind, so artfully
was a frame which surrounded it disposed.
Leaving Father Francis in the charge of two
Sappers, with orders to knock him down if
he attempted to escape, or made any dis-

turbance.   Seymour despatched a messenger
to Strange to procure a carriage, and with
the remainder of the party, hastily descended
to the late chamber of horrors.   Sister Grace
had partially recovered her senses, and, with
some trouble and delay, she was conveyed to
the chapel.

The carriage arrived, and the rescued girl,
accompanied by Seymour, soon reached the
Hall, where Ella received her, and took her
under her care.

Nott, who stayed behind, in spite of the
tears and protestations of innocence on the
part of the sisters, conveyed the whole party
to the nearest police station, and handed
them over to the Inspector, on a charge
of attempted murder.   They were brought
before the Hampshire Bench two days subsequently, but were remanded until Sister
Grace was well enough to appear against
them.

This time had not arrived when the next
fortnight had passed away.   Her evidence
was, therefore, taken in private, and upon it
the sisters were released, and Father Francis,

the Abbess, and the "unknown"—a prior of an Italian convent—with the executioners, were fully committed for trial at the ensuing Winchester Assizes, on a charge of attempted murder.

For some months Sister Grace was in a most precarious state, but time finally restored her to her fond relatives. The trial at length came on; but the prosecution, though conducted by an able and rising barrister, completely broke down—to the intense disgust of Seymour, Nott, and their numerous friends—for Father Francis adduced indisputable evidence that it had never been intended *really* to murder Grace. The back of the niche in which she had been immured was moveable; and although the sisters would of course (as was desired) have believed that she perished in her living tomb, she would eventually have been secretly removed from England into an Italian convent. What would have become of her *there* we will not attempt to imagine.

Our readers will probably have discovered that "the woman in black," whom Ella

encountered at Place House, was none other
than the lay sister she had rescued from
Emperor, and whom Seymour and Fordbrad
had succoured in Jamaica. She was aware
of Sister Grace's escape and capture, and had
guessed her probable fate. Gratitude to her
benefactors strove with the dread of being
discovered by Father Francis; but gratitude
triumphed, and from her the warnings had
emanated, and she had penned and delivered
the letter which Seymour at day-break had
received.

The situation of Sister Grace was therein
detailed, and a clue given to the spot whence
the dungeon might be entered. Luckily,
Seymour knew the locality, and what was
better, possessed the Ordnance Survey of the
district, on that most valuable, the 25 inch
scale. A ravine ran parallel, or nearly so,
to the convent and grounds. Nott and
Seymour made a scrutinizing reconnoissance
of the defile, and lighted upon a passage,
branching from its rocky side, and seeming
to run under the convent. They judged
(and rightly) that if this passage did not lead

to the looked for site, it would take them very near it. Not a moment was lost as human life was at stake. The company of Engineers were set to work with pickaxe and shovel. From eight A.M. till midnight they unceasingly toiled, burrowing among the accumulated *debris* of centuries. They were almost in despair, and nearly dead with fatigue, when the formost miner let fall his torch, and the party was in darkness. Strong gleams of yellow light pierced the blackness; they were near the goal! They heard the sound of Sister Grace's executioners at their fiendish work, and paused in surprise. One more bold stroke, and that a strong one—the cavern wall was breached, and the underground city captured.

CHAPTER XXII.

CONCLUSION.

" I loved thee for the gentle smile, that like a sunny ray
  Would steal around thy lovely lips whene'er my heart was
      gay ;
  I loved thee in thy sadness, when the joyous smile had fled,
  And left me but the mem'ry of the warmth its light once
      shed.
  I loved thee for thy beauty, like the violets, that bloom
  So sweetly 'neath the hawthorn hedge, in shadow and in
      gloom.
  So was it with thy loveliness ; it sought no brilliant sphere,
  But e'er could make the wildest waste a paradise appear.
  I loved thee when dark winter came, and at the social hearth
  It was thy voice that woke the tones of music and of mirth ;
  And when sometimes in gladsome mood, you sing the same
      sweet strain,
  I feel as if some dream had passed, and thou wert young
      again.
  And still I fondly love thee, tho' thy youth has passed away,
  And Time's unsparing hand hath tinged each glossy curl
      with grey ;
  Yes ! love thee fondly now, as when thine eye's dark meaning
      glance,
  First charm'd this wild and wayward heart beyond all
      utterance."   LANGHORNE.

THE summer and winter had come and gone ;

but it was not until the return of spring that Grace recovered her health and spirits, her elastic step, and bright smile. Nott was a constant visitor at the Hall; his feelings towards Grace had undergone but little change; he still looked forward to a time when his patience should receive its reward; but he did not seek to disturb her serenity by any marked attention, or display of feeling; he loved her too well to cause her uneasiness, and she soon ceased to feel any restraint in his presence. But the course of events urged him on, and compelled him at length to seek to end this suspense. His turn for foreign service was drawing near; he expected soon to be ordered abroad, and he resolved to try his fortune once more; it might be in vain, but he agreed with the great man who has written :——

> " It is better to have loved and lost
> Than never to have loved at all."

So he came over to Strange one sunny afternoon, and on inquiring for Miss Rivers heard she had gone to the old garden. He

Q 2

proceeded thither in search of her, and
followed the windings of the wall which led
through the wood, until he came to an opening surrounded by fantastic old trees—oak
and elm, and beech, and horse-chestnut, just
bursting into flower. The cawing of the
noisy rooks over their young broods; the
cooing of the wood pigeon; the call of the
heron; the sound of the rushing river; the
warbling of innumerable birds, and the cease-
less hum of insects, filled the little glade with
joyous sights and sounds that at another time
Nott would have stopped to contemplate with
a thankful spirit; but now his heart was filled
with other thoughts, and he passed rapidly
on. He had made up his mind what to do,
and nothing earthly would now have turned
him from his purpose. A few more steps, and
he perceived the object of his search. In a
rustic arbour, covered with creepers, in wild,
unpruned luxuriance, Grace was resting on
a low seat; her dark dress fell in graceful
folds around her, her hat was thrown aside,
and Ella's little child—the counterpart of her
mother—was standing at her knee, her hand

laid lightly and caressingly round Grace's neck, her golden hair gleaming in the sunlight, and shading her fair young face. Grace's lap was filled with wild flowers, and she was weaving a garland for May's tiny hat, while the child watched her quick fingers with infantine delight. Nott paused to gaze upon the picture; May saw him, and smiled a welcome. Miss Rivers, too, looked up; their eyes met. The glance was not encouraging; but Nott, remembering that 'faint heart never won fair lady,' heeded it not; he went into the arbour, and controlling his emotion as well as he could, sat down at her side, chatting away gaily on any subject rather than on the one which occupied the thoughts of both. At last the wreath was completed, and Grace rose to go.

"Forgive me, Miss Rivers, if I seek to detain you," he said; "my time here is short, the days of my stay are numbered; will you, can you, try to forget the past, and be to me what I have once already dared to ask? Forget all I did for you last year; any other officer, any gentleman, would have endeavoured to protect a lady in danger."

Grace was much agitated; she remembered but too vividly the solemn vow she had voluntarily taken, and of which Nott had been a witness. She had not yet made up her mind that she was not bound to act upon it as far as circumstances would permit. She was also afraid of being carried away by feelings, which, unconsciously to herself, were becoming deeper every day, and she was still somewhat trammelled by the superstition in which she had been reared. Her honest nature shrunk from the prospect of making new promises till fully assured she was at liberty to do so.

Nott watched her speaking countenance, and read the struggle in her mind; at last she answered :—

"I fear you will think I am ungrateful; but you know the manner in which I am already pledged; your happiness will always be dear to me; do not urge me to act against my conscience, but think of me kindly, if you can."

" How can you dwell upon that awful scene," he promptly replied, " or think that a vow wrung from you when under a false excitement of feeling, by the persuasion of a Romish monk—made voluntarily, it is true, but an unholy vow for all that—ought to be adhered to. Have you not from childhood been the slave of Rome's craft; can you really believe that a vow to do wrong ought to be kept? Look through your Bible, see what one of the early books tell of the vows of a young unmarried girl. Can an unholy vow be acceptable to God? Did not our Saviour condemn the Pharisees for not assisting indigent parents by the plea of the Corhan? Surely you will admit that the gospel teaching points out that the commandments of God are not to be made second to the tradition of men."

" No, Captain Nott," Miss Rivers replied, " I cannot quite see things in that light; as a friend whom I love, as a friend to whom I owe my life, I shall ever be glad to meet you; and if you go abroad, for your safety and

happiness I will pray, but I cannot say more ;
think kindly of me if you can."

Upon the whole, Nott was hopeful as to the
issue of his suit, but he wisely refrained from
pressing it further at the time ; so, lifting
little May, who said she was tired, in his
arms, they pursued their way to the house in
silence.

Nott's expectations were not disappointed ;
Grace had studied with an earnest mind the
pages of inspiration now first opened to her ;
she sought counsel and instruction ; and ere
long the mists of prejudice and ignorance
were cleared away, and she was able to look
calmly and thankfully on past trials, and
forward to the new life offered to her, with
its hopes and its duties.

Not long after, Grace accompanied her
husband to the Mauritius. Seymour and
Ella watched their departure with mingled
feelings ; and as the former lifted his little
daughter in his arms to wave a last farewell to
the departing friends, he felt that he realised
in himself the picture of human felicity, which
has been drawn by a master's hand. He was

possessed of competence, married to the woman of his choice, and with a fairy likeness of his wife in the person of his little daughter. Ella gazed long and sadly after them as they drove down the avenue; it was snapping another link in the chain of her entangled life.

We refrain from prolonging our tale to the usual extent of a three volume novel, more especially as public attention is now directed to the convent system in the United Kingdom.

We might have told at length of the gay wedding of Nott and Grace; how our old friends Mr. Fitz and Mr. Fordbrad were present, how the former (who was best man) ably represented the feelings of the ten bridesmaids, and *very nearly* followed Captain Nott's example of proposing to one of them, then and there. We might also narrate how the soldiers who had rescued Grace came to the ceremony, how the band played, " Haste to the wedding," and how both young and old made merry on that joyous summer day. We *did* think of carrying our readers with Captain and Mrs. Nott to their distant destination, and of dilating further upon Seymour's and Ella's married life, and perhaps glancing at Mr. Stanley in his bachelor's lodgings in Paris. We feel, however, it is better to leave our friends in the midst of their well merited happiness, and speak no more of their enemies. We have long followed their fortunes, and think we could not now do better than bid them all farewell.

Should we turn one more page who can tell what destiny might unfold.

THE END.

ADDENDA.

ADDENDA.

N.B.——This paragraph arrived too late for insertion in its proper place.

It is a melancholy fact, that the prediction contained in Seymour's and Ella's letters of yellow fever returning to Bermuda—letters originally written by the author, and published some years ago in the *Bermuda Royal Gazette* — is now being fearfully fulfilled. We have learned from various sources, particularly from a paragraph in the *Dublin Daily Express*, of 2nd September, " that the yellow fever has this season broken out with great virulence at Bermuda, and has made a great deal of havoc among the troops and civilians stationed there, numbers of whom, both officers and men, have fallen victims to the disease. One consequence has been a call for medical assistance from all the military surgeons now in Canada, and a number of them have left for Portland *en route* for Halifax, from whence they will proceed to Bermuda." The fever has, doubtless, been imported into Bermuda from Nassau. Yellow fever decimated Bermuda in (Welhent) 1780, again in 1818—19, once more in 1843, and again in 1853, when the last cases of the fearful epedimic more resembled the " Black Death " than any known form of disease. In 1856 and 1859 it appeared in milder form, dubbed by some wiseacres, " bilious intermittent fever," better, however, known in the colony as " yellow fever." And now we have the depressing intelligence that the terrible scourge is once more pursuing its course.

It is also not unworthy of remark, that Convent Life has within the last few days been the subject of two "leaders " in a well-known and wide-spread paper, *The Daily Telegraph ;* but the pages of this work were too far advanced to permit the author to avail himself of the hints they contained. The threat of conveying Ella to an Italian convent can hardly be considered to have been overdrawn, when we read in the *The Daily Telegraph*, of 10th September, a letter signed " N. M." The writer was taking a walk on the pier at Dover, and "met two nuns carrying by main force a beautiful girl, of from sixteen to eighteen, to the Ostend boat. She was dragged along by head and feet. When they had got her on board she shouted and screamed again."

" She was taken below as soon as possible, and the writer saw her no more. " I wondered " he or she relates, " if the girl was being taken against her wish to some dismal convent, which if one may judge from the company she was in, seemed likely. Was she insane? The intelligence I saw in her countenance gave no indication of insanity. I shall be pleased if any person who was present can throw any light on so sad a picture, which I turned from with an aching heart."

Im TheStory
personalised classic books

"Beautiful gift.. lovely finish.
My Niece loves it, so precious!"

Helen R Brumfieldon

★★★★★

UNIQUE GIFT

FOR KIDS, PARTNERS
AND FRIENDS

Timeless books such as:

Kids

Alice in Wonderland · The Jungle Book · The Wonderful Wizard of Oz
Peter and Wendy · Robin Hood · The Prince and The Pauper
The Railway Children · Treasure Island · A Christmas Carol

Adults

Romeo and Juliet · Dracula

Highly Customizable   **Change** Books Title   **Replace** Characters Names with yours   **Upload** Photo Inside pages   **Add** Inscriptions

Visit
Im TheStory .com
and order yours today!

CPSIA information can be obtained
at www.ICGtesting.com
Printed in the USA
BVHW041804220819
556561BV00022B/5221/P